MW00620817

Cesare and Lucrezia Borgia

To my Grandad, John Morris.
For your support, and for telling me how proud you were.
Wherever you are, I hope you have a copy of this book.
Rest in Peace.

Cesare and Lucrezia Borgia

Brother and Sister of History's Most Vilified Family

Samantha Morris

PEN & SWORD
HISTORY

First published in Great Britain in 2020 by
Pen & Sword History
An imprint of
Pen & Sword Books Ltd
Yorkshire – Philadelphia

Copyright © Samantha Morris 2020

ISBN 978 1 52672 440 3

The right of Samantha Morris to be identified as Author of this work
has been asserted by her in accordance with the Copyright, Designs
and Patents Act 1988.

A CIP catalogue record for this book is
available from the British Library.

All rights reserved. No part of this book may be reproduced or
transmitted in any form or by any means, electronic or mechanical
including photocopying, recording or by any information storage and
retrieval system, without permission from the Publisher in writing.

Typeset by Mac Style
Printed and bound in the UK by TJ Books,
Padstow, Cornwall.

Pen & Sword Books Limited incorporates the imprints of Atlas,
Archaeology, Aviation, Discovery, Family History, Fiction, History,
Maritime, Military, Military Classics, Politics, Select, Transport,
True Crime, Air World, Frontline Publishing, Leo Cooper, Remember
When, Seaforth Publishing, The Praetorian Press, Wharncliffe
Local History, Wharncliffe Transport, Wharncliffe True Crime
and White Owl.

For a complete list of Pen & Sword titles please contact

PEN & SWORD BOOKS LIMITED
47 Church Street, Barnsley, South Yorkshire, S70 2AS, England
E-mail: enquiries@pen-and-sword.co.uk
Website: www.pen-and-sword.co.uk

Or

PEN AND SWORD BOOKS
1950 Lawrence Rd, Havertown, PA 19083, USA
E-mail: Uspen-and-sword@casematepublishers.com
Website: www.penandswordbooks.com

Contents

Acknowledgments

The writing of this book has taken years and has truly taken me on an incredible journey. However none of this could not have been possible without the help of some wonderful individuals, to who I owe a great deal of thanks.

First of all I would like to say thank you to the incredibly helpful staff at the Vatican Archives who helped me locate various documents and books. Whilst I did not have the opportunity to visit the archives in person, the staff pointed me in the direction of various sources both held in their online archives and elsewhere in the public domain.

A special thank you goes to my partner, Matt, for his love and again his patience whilst I have worked on this gargantuan project. He has been with me every step of the way and listened to me babble on about the Borgia family from dawn till dusk and visiting places associated with the Borgia without even a grumble. In fact, he has grown to love the family almost as much as I do!

The support of my family has been invaluable during my writing. My mum and dad have been so supportive in my endeavours, from the moment I first said I wanted to write a history book. I would also like to extend a heartfelt thank you to my grandad, John Morris, to whom this book is dedicated. The day before he passed we had a long conversation about my writing work and he told me how he had copies of my previous work and that he was looking forward to reading this one when it came out. This book is for you, Grandad, and I hope wherever you are that you enjoy reading it.

I would also like to extend a very special thank you to Pen and Sword publishing for taking a chance with this book and for their support and guidance through this whole process.

And finally, thank you to everyone who has supported me on this endeavour. There are far too many of you to name, but thank you for reading my work and encouraging me to continue on this incredible journey.

Samantha Morris
Southampton, 2019

Introduction

Just beyond the Raphael Rooms in the Vatican Museums are the Borgia apartments – today these rooms house a modern art exhibition looked down upon by the murals of Pinturrichio and the faces of the Borgia family. The rooms are often not as busy as the rest of the museums as they are off the beaten track, only really available for visitors if you go searching for them once you've fought your way through the crowded Sistine chapel. Guided tours, however, will often take their groups through the rooms and talk about what they, and most people who know of the Borgia family, believe to be the truth. In much the same way as the Beefeaters at the Tower of London tell the story that Anne Boleyn was brought in through Traitor's Gate (she wasn't), the Tour Guides tell their groups that the Borgia family committed myriad crimes including the one of incest. Murder, poison and corruption also feature highly in their tales of the family and two names often come up – Cesare and Lucrezia Borgia. Their faces gaze down upon the tourists from the beautiful murals within the Room of the Saints, part of a number of rooms that made up Alexander VI's secret apartments within the Apostolic Palace, and one can only imagine how these two individuals would feel if they knew the rumours started by their enemies were still spoken about in our modern times as if they were fact, rather than what they were; vicious gossip and hearsay.

The stories that are told not only by the tour guides of the Vatican but also by modern day media must have come from somewhere. Indeed, the family was surrounded by enemies who disliked the sheer power held by a family of Spaniards. Italy at the time was rife with xenophobia as well as jealousy – if another family could not get what they wanted out of the Borgia family, then they would quickly turn on them, dripping poisonous rumours into the ears of everyone who would listen. During the time of the Borgias, Italy as a country did not exist but rather was made up of a conglomeration of separate states that were ruled by their own princes, some of whom gave their allegiance to the Pope whilst others ruled only for themselves. These rulers were often incredibly powerful families – for instance the Sforza family ruled Milan and the Medici ruled Florence until they were deposed by Florentine signoria and the monk Savonarola. Other states were under the dominion of other European powers – Mantua, ruled by the Gonzaga, was a fiefdom of the Holy Roman Empire whilst other areas such as Ferrara were allies of France and Naples to Spain. Italy as a unified nation state did not come into being until 1861 and in June 1946, Italy abolished its monarchy altogether after a referendum was held.

One can only imagine the conversations that were whispered throughout the courts of Europe throughout the Borgia Papacy, poison dripped into the ears of anyone who wanted to believe that the most powerful family in the Catholic world were caught up in all sorts of scandal. Rumours abounded of incest and sexual intrigue, of fratricide and poisoning. And at the centre of these rumours, along with the Pope, two names were a constant. Cesare and Lucrezia Borgia, brother and sister, were said to be lovers. Lucrezia was said to poison her enemies whilst Cesare's name was whispered in fear.

Even after his death in 1507, Cesare Borgia's name was synonymous with evil. His sister, despite becoming more and more pious as the years went on, was still accused of sexual intrigue. These ideas about the most famous siblings in Renaissance history have stuck and have come down to us today. But the question is, why have they remained in the public imagination? Where did the hatred come from? Where did the rumours of incest stem from?

These are questions that have fascinated me since my interest in the Borgia family first began. In modern day adaptations of the historical record on television and in novels, you still see Cesare and Lucrezia being portrayed as incestuous intriguers. But why? If you dig a little deeper, the answers to these questions can be found in the historical record. And, as with the vilification of other noble families and royalty in both earlier and later years, you can find that these are all based on spurious rumour and propaganda created with one simple end in sight. To destroy the reputation of those in question. Even then, for the longest time, historians have gone with the idea that the Borgia family are evil. It is only recently that historians have begun to question these ideas.

It is my aim, throughout this book, to tell the story of history's most maligned siblings. As we will see, the real story is so much more fascinating than the tale fabricated by their enemies. And it is my hope that by telling this story, it will help disperse the idea that the Borgia siblings were evil incarnate, and show that Cesare and Lucrezia were nothing more than people.

To begin, we must examine the world, and the family, into which Cesare and Lucrezia were born. Renaissance Italy was a complicated place, a country made up of warring states ruled over by their own leaders who were, in a way, like monarchs. This world, as well as the family name, would define both siblings from their birth until their deaths.

This is the story of Cesare and Lucrezia Borgia, history's most notorious siblings.

Chapter 1

The Rise of The Borgias: A Background

In the small town of Borja, near Zaragoza in Spain, there were a large number of households who used the name 'de Borja'. Many were prominent and wealthy landowners, nobility in a way, whereas others were not so wealthy. It was in this town that Alonso de Borja was born on 31 December 1378, to a branch of the de Borja family that today would be classed as the middle working class. They certainly were not the poorest branch of the family, nor were they the richest. But the name bore considerable weight in the area, and those who carried the name proudly stated that they could trace their lineage back to the Aragonese rulers of history.

Born to Domenico de Borja, a landowner of the Torre Canal branch of the family, and Francina Marti, Alonso would go on to spend the majority of his life as a member of lesser orders within the Church and was, predominantly, a lawyer. His career began, as did that of many clerics within the church, at an early age – at the age of fourteen in 1392 he was sent to the University of Lerida where he studied both civil and canon law. Alonso excelled in both subjects despite not being particularly intellectual. Alonso ended up staying at the university to earn his doctorate in the same subject and by the time he finished his studies, he was given the opportunity to become a lecturer in the areas of study at which he had done so well. What is interesting here is that throughout his early career, Alonso was completely free of any scandal – something that his later family would never experience. He kept to himself, showed no interest in the Renaissance ideals that were sweeping across Europe like a whirlwind, yet still remained a deeply respected academic. It was this hard work that eventually brought him to the attention of Pope Benedict XIII who, in 1408, appointed Alonso to the diocese of Lerida. As with his studies, Alonso excelled at this post and just three years later, thanks to his efficiency and hard work, was promoted to Canon of Lerida cathedral.

At around this time, or perhaps a little earlier, Alonso apparently crossed paths with preacher, Vincente Ferrer. This Spanish friar was a famous figure within Valencia at the time, known for his methods of converting Jews to Christianity. Wherever he appeared, he attracted huge numbers of people who watched the friar as he preached and he also studied philosophy at the same university where Alonso studied law. When Ferrer and Alonso met, Ferrer is said to have made a great prophecy regarding the young cleric, claiming that Alonso would 'receive the highest office a man can hold; you will honour me after my death and I hope you will always live as virtuously as you do now'.[1] According to many, Alonso took the prophecy to heart. He can't have missed the allusion to the Papacy after all, and once he had been elevated to the College of Cardinals, waited patiently for his time to come.

In his late thirties, the scholarly and quiet young man was chosen to go as Lerida's representative to the Council of Constance. This council had been called as a method of dealing with one of the greatest and most damaging decades in the history of the Roman Catholic Church – the Great Schism, which had been a massive crisis of authority for well over forty years. In essence, the Great Schism meant that there had been a split of Papal Authority between Avignon, where the Papacy had moved in the early 1300s, and Rome – at times there had been two Popes, at others three. Despite the fact that in 1377 Papal authority had moved back to Rome, just one year later Pope Gregory XI was dead and six Cardinals were still resident in Avignon. The people of Rome desperately feared that a French Pope would be elected in place of an Italian and as such there was rioting outside of the Conclave that followed Gregory's death. Thankfully, at least in Roman eyes, an Italian was elected who took the name of Urban VI. It was Urban who began the schism, however, thanks to abusive behaviours that had many suspecting the Pope to be insane. The Cardinals publicly spoke out that his election had not been valid, ousted him from the throne of St Peter and instead chose a new Pope. This Pope, Clement VIII, took those Cardinals who supported him to Avignon where he set up a rival Papacy against Urban, who still held Rome.

For the next few decades, confusion reigned between both Avignon and Rome with no one knowing which Pope was the real one whilst different monarchs supported different Popes. There were attempts to bring the schism to an end, but the most promising came with the Council of Pisa in 1409, which unfortunately only led to a third line of claimants to the throne of St Peter. For many, three Popes was a step too far and so the Council of Constance was organised by Pope John XXIII. It was this council, begun in 1414, that Alonso de Borja joined as Lerida's representative. Whilst there is no evidence that Borja participated in any of the sessions at the Council, it is important to look at the Council as a whole as it left the future Pope, and loyal follower of the Church leaders, with questions that would eventually affect how he ran the Church of Rome.

One of the best accounts of the Council of Constance comes from Ulrich Von Richental, a citizen of Constance and the son of a municipal scribe who evidently had an educated upbringing and was incredibly privileged. In the account, he claims that he was an eye witness to many of the most important sessions within the Council – as such he must have had some influence to gain access to these events. Richental states that the Pope arrived in Constance in 1414 with a massive retinue, entering the town on 27 October accompanied by six hundred people including eight Cardinals and some of the greatest Humanists of the time. The town became so overcrowded thanks to various tradespeople showing up to ply their crafts at such a huge event that tents had to be set up to accommodate all of the visitors – the locals complained of the salesmen coming in, saying that they would lose out on business if the foreigners were allowed to continue, but the Council stated that trade was free and so permission was granted for anyone to sell their wares. More people flooded through the town gates every day, contributing to the overcrowding and Richental notes amusingly that, 'Should I mention every person this book would get too fat'.[2]

The overcrowding within the town got so much that the council officials had to bring in certain controls. Already noted are the permissions for trading, but as well as this they staged public executions in an effort to curb the crime that would be rife at such an overcrowded event. Controls on the quality of service for visitors were also brought in, including the instructions that tablecloths and sheets should be cleaned and changed every fourteen days.[3]

The main aim of the Council was, of course, to end the Great Schism that had been plaguing the Catholic Church for decades. However, there were other aims that needed to be dealt with at the same time – the issue of ecclesiastical governance (which was linked to the schism), and the issue around the suppression of heresy. And it was the heresy issue that Pope John XXIII tried desperately to use to his advantage, turning the attention away from ending the schism and the complaints about his own thuggish corruption towards getting rid of a man by the name of Jan Hus.

Hus, a man who had been a thorn in the side of the Church for a long time, had been granted safe passage to the Council so he could stand before them and explain his behaviour and views to them. Hus had boldly spoken out against the abuses of the Church and stated that the highest power was the Holy Scripture rather than just one man – according to Hus the Papacy, as a human institution, could not possibly be infallible. Men, and as such Popes, would commit sin and so any immoral Pope should be judged by his Church colleagues and stripped of his offices. These teachings were seen as heresy by the Church and Hus was excommunicated. He refused to submit to the orders of the Church that he stop his heretical teachings. But the safe passage granted to Hus by Emperor Sigismund was ignored. Hus was arrested on 3 November without trial, despite the assurances of his safety, and thrown into a cell. He was denied the chance to speak before the Council, even when he fell seriously ill and asked that someone be appointed to speak on his behalf.[4] Hus was put to death on 6 July 1415 by being burned at the stake.

Yet the man who wanted to use Hus as a distraction from ending the Great Schism had, in the interim, been deposed. He fled from the very council that he had called for after his supporters had turned against him and demanded that he be put on trial for his many crimes against the Church. John XXIII disguised himself as a stable boy and left Constance during a jousting tournament held in Emperor Sigismund's honour – it was his aim to reach the safety of the Duke of Burgundy's lands across the River Rhine. But by the point of his escape, 20 March 1416, people were already calling out for John's abdication. Emperor Sigismund, the main power behind the Council, sent his soldiers out after John to arrest him. During the Pope's flight, he was tried in his absence and found guilty of multiple crimes against the Church as well as rape, sodomy and incest. Now formally deposed, he spent the next four years in the custody of Elector Ludwig III of Bavaria. It was only when John paid Ludwig a vast sum that his freedom was given and he was forgiven by the Church of Rome for his crimes.[5]

Even as the Council of Constance elected Martin V, it demanded that the new Pope be subject to their authority, as they were the highest authority in the Church. Martin believed that it was the Pope who had supreme authority, yet still the Council demanded that he be under their control. It was around this point, probably spurred on by what he had witnessed during the Council, that Borja began to question what he had seen – the man had always been loyal to those who ruled the Church and so he stated that Church unity was needed, although without the Pope as supreme head even over the council, such unity was an impossible task. It was a view that he would constantly keep throughout his ecclesiastical career.

Following on from the Council of Constance, with the deposition of John XXIII and Benedict XIII along with the election of Pope Gregory XII (who lived for only a year) and Martin V in 1417, the schism was 'officially' over. Alonso de Borja turned his attention to other matters – at the age of around forty he made his first visit to the court of Alfonso V who would end up playing a huge part in Borja's life. Borja was offered permanent employment at Alfonso's court as secretary to the king, which would have given him almost constant access to the young monarch, and he jumped at the opportunity. Now, at the very centre of European affairs, his way was paved to the Cardinalate and eventually the Papacy.

Borja's career with the Aragonese royal family went from strength to strength and in 1420, he was elected as Vice Chancellor to the Regency. This meant that whilst Alfonso was absent fighting in Sardinia and Corsica, Borja would rule in his stead. During this time, despite the Council of Constance officially 'ending' the Great Schism, there were still other claimants to the Papal throne. When Martin V returned to Rome, Alfonso V reaffirmed his support for Clement VIII, a Spanish Cardinal of the Avignon curia. At the same time, Queen Joanna of Naples had given her support to the French king – Borja had hoped desperately for the two to reconcile after a long war between them, but now his hopes were dashed. Joanna stated that Alfonso was no longer her heir, but Louis of Anjou was. It would be the beginning of a bitter fight for Naples that would last for years.[6]

Eventually Alfonso gave in and admitted that Martin was probably the true Pope rather than Clement. In 1429, Borja then took it upon himself to visit the remote town of Peniscola, where Benedict XIII had died, to speak with Clement. Borja offered Clement the bishopric of Palma in Mallorca if only he would step down as 'Pope' and submit himself to the Papacy in Rome. Clement agreed and so Alonso de Borja did what the Council of Constance could not. The Great Schism was now officially over, and clerical power returned fully to Rome. Martin V was so grateful for Alonso's work that he was made the Bishop of Valencia – the home diocese of the Borgia family, and an incredibly rich episcopal see. As such, Borja was able to help his family and brought his widowed sister and their children into the huge palace that came with the post. It should be noted that up until this point, Borja had never once been ordained as a priest. He had been happy to remain on the lower rungs of the ecclesiastical ladder, but now that he had been made a bishop he had to take that step. For the next few years, Borja would watch as all his hard work during the reign of Martin fell into wrack and ruin – Martin died in 1431 and was succeeded by Gabriele Condulmer who became Eugenius IV.

Upon Euguenius' ascension to the throne of St Peter, the Council of Basel was formally opened – previously it had been demanded that Martin V open the Council or be deposed. But his death meant that the new Pope had little choice but to open the much demanded council. Six months later however, Eugenius decided that he wouldn't be controlled by a Council when he was supposed to be God's representative on earth. He closed the council and it was one of the biggest mistakes that he would ever make. Whilst the turnout of the Council of Basel had been incredibly sparse, those who did attend stated that the Pope had absolutely no authority over them and – instead of them being dismissed – they completely withdrew the Bull of Dissolution that Eugenius had presented to them and demanded that unless he presented himself to them, he would be the one being dismissed from his post.[7] It was only when Emperor Sigismund stepped in that the deadlock between Eugenius and the Council was ended. Eugenius was forced to withdraw his Bull and to submit to the council. Sadly for Eugenius, however, this was not enough for his enemies, the Colonna and the people of Rome. They rose up against him in 1434 and demanded that the city be made into a republic. Eugenius was forced to flee the city dressed as a monk – he was identified quickly as he sailed down the Tiber in a little boat and left Rome under a barrage of sticks and stones.[8] Although still officially Pope, the Council announced that Eugenius was a heretic and elected another anti-Pope – yet again, Alonso de Borja's hard work was ruined.

Alfonso V showed friendliness towards the Council of Basel and their new anti-Pope, Felix V. It is not hard to imagine how irritated Alonso must have been over this. He had, after all, worked hard to end the schism and worked to convince his master that the Roman Popes were the rightful heirs of St Peter. Despite this, he still worked alongside Alfonso as his secretary and even oversaw the education of Alfonso's illegitimate son, Ferrante. Despite still working for Alfonso, Borja was starting to show his chagrin towards his master and his working closely with Basel – he refused to go as Alfonso's envoy to Basel and instead chose to fully show his support to Pope Eugenius. When Eugenius ordered the Council of Basel to go to Ferrara and then to Florence in 1438, Alonso de Borja made the decision to go to Florence himself to show his support.

Between the years of 1438 and 1444, Borja's fortunes changed forever. Now, at over sixty years old, Alonso de Borja had climbed his way up the ecclesiastical ladder to the post of Bishop of Valencia and had worked closely with King Alfonso V of Aragon. He was only to climb higher, much as Ferrer had prophesied so many years ago.

During the 1430s, Alfonso lost a battle and became the prisoner of Duke Fillipo Maria Visconti. Yet, to his credit and with incredible logic, Alfonso managed to talk his way out of his imprisonment by convincing Visconti that with French power in Naples, it meant that Milan would be pressed from all sides. It would be better for Naples to be ruled by the Aragonese, surely? Visconti agreed and sent Alfonso on his way, where the Aragonese ruler ended up sending the French running from Naples and leaving the way open for him to finally claim his throne.[9] Of course, Alfonso could not formally take the crown of Naples without Papal recognition, and yet again it came down to Alonso de Borja to sort things out. By convincing Alfonso V (I of Naples) and Pope Eugenius to look past their differences, he showed them that they could achieve far more by working together than against each other. Felix V tried desperately to show Alfonso that he could invest him as King of Naples but the anti-Pope, as well as the Council of Basel, had so little standing anywhere at this point that there really was little point in him trying. Borja represented Alfonso in the negotiations and the outcome was that Alfonso formally recognised Eugenius as Pope whilst Alfonso was formally invested as King of Naples and recognised as such by the Church of Rome. Just as he had done at the end of Martin V's reign, Alonso de Borja had ended a period of turmoil within the Church. It was something for him to be proud of and, in thanks for his hard work and in pure recognition for his services towards the Church, Pope Eugenius made him a Cardinal.

Granted the lands and church of Santi Quattro Coronati on Rome's Coelian Hill, Borja formally took up residence in the Eternal City in 1445. It should be noted that even when he had been granted a Cardinal's hat, Cardinal Borja, or Borgia as his name had now come to be Italianised, he made sure that not an ounce of scandal came to be associated with his name. He was now in his early sixties and kept away from the politics and machinations of his royal master, instead preferring to spend his time in the gardens of his palace and giving charitably. When Eugenius died in 1447, at the Conclave that followed there was no mention of Borgia ever being considered to succeed him, nor of him being involved in the politics and scheming that happened at every single Papal Conclave. Perhaps Ferrer had been wrong in his prophecy – after all, Borgia was getting older and seemingly wanted to have a quiet life well away from any sort of political machinations.

But everything was to change in 1455. Eugenius' successor, Nicholas V, had been the one to begin to bring Rome back to the glory it had once had. Although a small and withered old man, he was determined to bring the Church in line with the secular culture of the Renaissance that had been sweeping Italy. He had proclaimed that 1450 would be a holy year and the huge number of pilgrims that flooded into Rome meant that Nicholas had been able to bank 100,000 golden sovereigns and continue with his work to restore the city. He also moved the official Papal residence from the Lateran to the Vatican Palace. According to Piccolomini, the Cardinal of Siena, by the time of his death in 1455 he had started far more than he had finished.[10] He would never see Rome turn from the 'rubbish heap of history' back into the beautiful centre of Christendom.

The result of 1455's Conclave was to be a surprise to everyone. As was usual in Papal Conclaves, threats and arguing were rife – along with political scheming – and there was no way at all to break the deadlock between the Orsini and the Colonna family. So how on earth could the Cardinals locked within the Vatican come up with a compromise to their problem? They had to make sure that they elected someone who would not live long and who wouldn't cause any issues for any of them when it came to gaining more power. In the end, they settled on the idea of an elderly man who could be used as a puppet – two names came forward, although much to the chagrin of those locked within they were both Spaniards. Ideally they wanted an Italian Pope, but in this case the best and seemingly most pliable option was the quiet Bishop of Valencia. Alonso de Borja was elected as Pope Calixtus III and finally Ferrer's prophecy for the man had come true. There was no more waiting for the man who had come from the little Valencian town. He had climbed to the highest office in Christendom, and he would make sure he made use of it.

Calixtus was not to be the submissive Pope that everyone hoped he would be. Thanks to what he had seen during the Great Schism, he knew what it would take to make sure that the Papacy remained in control. He who had raised the Borgia family from obscurity also raised others within his family to special favours within the Church – this was not particularly surprising as every Pope up until that point had done so, and would continue to do so long after his death. Three of his nephews were raised within the church. Two of them were made Cardinals before the age of thirty, Rodrigo Borgia being granted the post of Vice Chancellor, whilst the third nephew, Pedro Luis, was given the title of Captain General of the Papal armies and given the sprawling castle of the Castel Sant Angelo. Whilst giving such favours was not unusual, thanks to the Romans' dislike of Spaniards and in particular Catalans like the Borgias, it caused widespread dissent.[11] It was a pattern that would be seen constantly throughout the reign of the Borgia dynasty, their Catalan background being used against them in xenophobic attacks.

During his reign, Calixtus was intent on saving Christendom from the Turks and began to work on sending a Crusade over to Constantinople. He stripped the Vatican library just before his coronation, demanding that the gold and silver bindings that covered manuscripts be removed in order to finance his holy war. He even had the magnificent tombs of two bodies, found in a crypt beneath the church of Saint Petronilla

in 1458, stripped of their gold and silver linings – it was melted down
and put into the Crusade fund, giving Calixtus over 1000 ducats to put
into the war effort.[12] The Crusade ended in failure however, and the
people had had enough of crusades, knowing that so many before had
failed miserably. Even the great European powerhouses refused to help
for the most part – Henry VI could not help as the Wars of the Roses
were starting to get underway and taking up all of England's time and
manpower. Even Francesco Sforza, the ruler of Milan, would not help.
The thirty ships promised by France ended up staying at home to help
protect King Charles VII and his kingdom against any potential English
threats.[13] Calixtus did manage to send troops out but despite naval
victories against the Turks in July of 1456, off the coast of Belgrade, and
in 1457 off the island of Lesbos, it all came to nothing.[14]

The Borgia family were in the ascendant and even though Calixtus'
reign would only last a few short years, the family would stay at the centre
stage of Italian politics for decades to come. The Borgias who came
down to us through history really began with the rise of Rodrigo Borgia
to the Cardinalate, thanks to the machinations of his uncle. Throughout
his career in the church, he would prove himself to be intelligent, an
astute politician and manipulative to the extreme – qualities that any
man within the Church needed at that point.

The summer of 1458 was a stifling one and, as happened almost
every year in the Eternal City , the season brought with it the diseases
of malaria and plague. Calixtus became seriously unwell. At the age of
eighty, after being ailing and feeble almost since the day he was elected
as Pope, it was only a matter of time until he succumbed. His nephews,
having heard that his health was failing and the aged Pope was close to
death, arrived at his bedside to keep him company in his last moments.
All about Rome rumour began to spread that the pontiff was dying, with
people beginning to make plans over how they could take advantage of
the Borgia Pope's passing. And of course, the Orsini and Colonna clans
planned to do their best to make sure they came out of the situation
on top. The people of Rome became murderous – their hatred of the

Catalans coming to the fore – even being a Spaniard in Rome was dangerous by this point with Spanish individuals being attacked in the streets and Spanish homes being burned to the ground. No one wanted another Spanish Pope and this was their way of telling the Curia, who felt the same way, that they wanted an Italian on the throne of St Peter. Things even got so bad that the majority of Calixtus' household left the city, leaving the ailing Pontiff to die alone.

Rodrigo Borgia, Cardinal and Vice Chancellor, refused to leave Rome and his uncle's side. Whilst other members of his family had fled, including Pedro Luis, Rodrigo remained steadfast in an incredibly brave move. His uncle passed away on 6 August 1458, just three years after his election, in a small dark room. His death was greeted by riots in the streets, as well as jubilation from the Curia. Despite his pious nature, his hard work to end the Great Schism and his fervour for ending the rule of Islam in Constantinople, Calixtus had been hated. And no one wanted another Spaniard as Pope.

With the death of Calixtus, it now became important for the Borgia Cardinal to hold on to everything that had been given to him and his family by his uncle. Rodrigo Borgia had to maintain the Spanish presence in the College of Cardinals, but he also had to remain almost out of sight to avoid any more hostility towards his family. It was during this time that Rodrigo Borgia proved himself to be astutely political and manipulative – it was as if he knew what to do to keep hold of the power that he had gained in the previous reign. His first full blown show of his incredible political mind was during the Conclave that followed his uncle's death. As previously mentioned, most of the Curia wished to stop the accession of another foreigner to the throne of St Peter – and during the Conclave, Cardinal Piccolomini was voted in by a procedure known as the accession. Sixteen Cardinals were locked within the Vatican and on the third day of voting he had gained nine votes, whilst the French Cardinal D'Estouville gained only six. That left one vote. It was Rodrigo Borgia who stood up and claimed that he acceded to the accession of Piccolomini, the Cardinal of Siena and, after a pause, each and every Cardinal locked within the Conclave declared that they too were for Piccolomini.[15] It was a clever move on Borgia's part, to side with an Italian Pope – he clearly knew that it would leave him in good stead for the future and that he would be able to keep hold of everything that he had gained during the reign of Calixtus.

In fact it was this exceptionally clever move that put Cardinal Rodrigo Borgia in great standing with the new Pope, Pius II. He would see a further three Popes elected before he himself gained the chance to ascend to the throne of St Peter, and throughout all of these reigns he would lead a charmed career as Vice Chancellor of the Holy See, amassing an incredible amount of wealth. Throughout his time, the handsome Cardinal would have a number of women fall under his spell – leading to him having two of his most famous mistresses during his later years. Rodrigo, as with other Cardinals, never made his sexual encounters a secret. After all, the vows of chastity that the priesthood swore to were flouted on a daily basis. Even Popes fathered illegitimate children. It was not a pattern that Rodrigo Borgia would ever break.

Sadly for Rodrigo, however, during one of his earliest missions for Pius II, stories of his amorous exploits would get back to the Pope. Borgia had been sent by Pius to make his native village into a bishopric and from February to April of 1459, Borgia was to be foreman of the project. Whilst here, the women of Siena fell under the spell of the handsome young Cardinal and once Pius heard about these exploits, he sent a stern letter of rebuke to the Cardinal.

'We are told that the dances were immodest and the seductions of love beyond bounds and that you yourself behaved as if you were one of the most vulgar young man of the age. In truth, I should blush as to set down in detail all I have been told of what happened. Not only these things themselves, but the mere mention of them, are a dishonour to the office you hold.'[16]

The letter goes on at length about Rodrigo's exploits in Siena, and one can tell from the very tone of the letter that it was written in a moment of anger. According to Pius, Borgia had become a 'laughing stock' thanks to his orgies, and his name was on the lips of everyone in Rome thanks to his scandalous behaviour. Yet Rodrigo explained away his actions, to receive a letter once more from Pius stating that his actions were 'less grave than I was first told'. Evidently the stories had been twisted out of proportion, or perhaps it was Rodrigo who twisted the truth to try and get out of being in trouble.

Nevertheless, Borgia still managed to remain close to Pius as his 'beloved Son', and continued to be involved heavily in Church politics. For instance, when Thomas of Morea came to Rome in 1461, Pius put Borgia in charge of having the Quattro Santi Coronati made fit for their visitors stay. When Morea left the relic of the head of St Andrew in the fortress of Narni, Borgia had it moved from there to the Vatican on 13 April and, using his love of ostentatious performance, had his home decorated to mark the occasion so that it outshone every other house on the route of the parade. This love of ostentation continued even after Pius died and other Popes took over the mantle. Cardinal Pietro Barbo, a close friend of Rodrigo's, was elected as Paul II – Paul, like Rodrigo, was a lover of luxury and had palaces built that would change the way Rome looked forever. With the building of the majestic Palazzo Venezia, the Renaissance had truly come to Rome. Paul even moved out of the Vatican into his new palace and it became the centre of court life in the Eternal City. The Vatican treasury was moved here and during carnival seasons, festivals were held within the palaces grounds. Paul's reign would be a spectacle in itself and one in which Rodrigo Borgia would find himself incredibly comfortable.[17]

Chapter 2

The Borgia Bastards

Throughout Rodrigo's time as Cardinal, he attracted the attention of the ladies. We already know of his dalliances with the ladies of Siena, but he also became involved with women in Rome. It was not unusual for the Princes of the Church to father children, and Rodrigo Borgia was no exception. Before the birth of his better known children, Rodrigo had fathered three by unknown mothers – Pedro Luis, Jeronima and Elisabetta. But the four children who have come down to us in history as part of the Borgia legend were born to Rodrigo's favoured mistress Vanozza Cattanei, the daughter of the celebrated artist Jacopo Pintoris. She was very likely to have been born in Rome, however there is some argument that she was in fact from Mantua. The reasoning behind this is because her last name Cattanei, or Cattaneo, is an incredibly common surname in the area. Some even point to her daughter Lucrezia's blonde hair as being proof that Vanozza is Mantuan rather than from Rome itself. But the Mantuan envoy at the court of the Borgia makes no mention of the Borgia children's mother having been from Mantua – surely had it been the case, such an attentive observer of the family would have immediately pointed it out in his dispatches? There is also a document dating to 1483 which states that her blood relatives are the sons of a certain Magister Antonio da Brescia, which potentially could mean that she was from the Brescia region of Northern Italy. It seems likely, therefore, that Vanozza Cattanei and her family weren't native Romans. Vanozza, the 'Roman woman' as mentioned in the secret bull of 1493 legitimising Cesare as the son of Pope Alexander VI, seems to simply have just been living in Rome at the time when her children by Rodrigo Borgia were conceived.[1] What is certain about Vanozza, however, is that she must have been both incredibly attractive as well as very strong willed to have caught the attention of Rodrigo and kept it for as long as she did. Rodrigo even arranged for her to have a marriage of convenience to the obscure Domenico Giannozzo di Rignano – a way of making sure that Vanozza kept her 'virtue' but at the same time allowing him to continue his affair with her. Domenico was happy enough with the arrangement, choosing to spend as much time travelling away from Rome on church business as he could.

It was at some point between September 1475 and April 1476 that Vanozza gave birth to a little boy and, despite the fact she was married to Domenico, it was clear to everyone that the child was not his. Vanozza Cattanei had been the mistress of Rodrigo Borgia for at least two years previously – everyone knew who the little boy's father was. The child was named Cesare Borgia, and would go down in history as one of the greatest warlords and most maligned men that the world had ever seen.

Vanozza gave birth to three more children whose paternity was attested to Rodrigo Borgia. Juan, often considered to be his favourite son, was born in 1476; Lucrezia in 1480 and Gioffre in 1481. Regarding Gioffre, Rodrigo Borgia contested whether or not he had actually fathered the child, as his relationship with Vanozza had long since cooled off – he had arranged another marriage for her after the death of Domenico in 1480, to Giorgio di Croce and believed Gioffre to have been fathered by Vanozza's new husband rather than himself. Yet she insisted that Gioffre was a Borgia and so Rodrigo took the boy fully into the family as his illegitimate son.[2] Vanozza gave birth to one more son, Ottaviano, who was the legitimate son of Di Croce. However, by 1486, both the child and his father were dead. Rodrigo hastily arranged for another marriage for his previous mistress and mother to his children, arranging for her to marry Carlo Canale, a man of little means who used his links with the Borgia family after his marriage to gain as much of a reputation as he possibly could. When Rodrigo became Pope, Canale benefitted greatly when he was made Governor of the Torre Di Nona. Vanozza, however, did not have much contact with her children – they were brought up away from her home as the children of a Cardinal and although Cesare remained close with her, her relationship with her daughter was, by all accounts, not an affectionate one.

Cesare and Juan were given their own households as befitted sons of a Prince of the Church whilst Lucrezia, the little girl who Rodrigo Borgia loved so dearly, was placed in the household of Adriana de Mila. De Mila was his cousin and evidently he believed that she would be the influence his daughter needed to be brought up in a manner befitting that of a noblewoman.

Even during their early lives, both Cesare and Lucrezia were already important pieces on their father's chessboard. Both were groomed for their specific uses – Cesare as a Prince of the Church and Lucrezia as a young woman who would enter into a political marriage. Both would, in their own way, end up taking control of their own destinies some years down the line.

Education was, of course, exceptionally important for the children of a man so high in the Church. Cesare would have begun his education at a very early age – although he was already fluent in Spanish (it was the principal language spoken around the family home), Cesare learned to read, write and speak Latin, Italian, Greek and French. He would also have been instructed in the classical works of Tacitus, Livy and Herodotus. It was from these classical works that he would have come to understand the idea of fortuna, something that was so important to him in his later life as a soldier who believed he embodied everything that Julius Caesar stood for – after all, he had been named after Caesar, and even signed himself using the Spanish equivalent of his name 'Cesar' throughout his life.[3] Both fortuna and virtu were elements that stuck with Cesare from his earliest days, and he would have believed that everything he did would lead to him shaping his own destiny. Fortuna was an element that Cesare would keep coming back to during his days as a soldier, long after he eventually threw off the crimson robes of the Cardinalate. As well as studying academically as a young man, Cesare's education concentrated on the physical – along with his academic study, he would consistently remain physically active throughout his life – with lessons including horsemanship hunting and, in time honoured Spanish tradition, bullfighting.

There are many contemporary accounts of the beauty of Rodrigo Borgia's children. Not only was Cesare's incredible academic prowess and sportsmanship mentioned time and time again, but also that he was an incredibly handsome young man whose body was 'well proportioned'. The Venetian ambassador even described Cesare as a man with a 'head most beautiful'.[4] Whilst there is no surviving contemporary portrait of Cesare, the one generally attested as being of him and labelled 'Dux Valentinus' shows a man full of confidence and a man who inherited much of his looks from his mother. What was already evident, even at a young age, was just how changeable Cesare's mood could be – to others he could be incredibly frank in his speech, not holding back his thoughts but inwardly he was secretive and devious. When he did have sporadic outbursts of enjoying any sort of activity, they were often followed with bouts of depression. Mixed in with this was the self-belief that he could make anything of himself if he so willed it, based on his belief in Fortuna and Virtu. Machiavelli later noted that he had 'confidence almost superhuman' and that he believed 'himself capable of accomplishing whatever he undertakes'.[5]

As for Lucrezia, the darling of the Borgia family, as a child she was described as tall for her age, with a long neck and luscious blonde locks. She was also forever smiling and laughing, full of gaiety and incredibly elegant. She had an incredible inner toughness about her demeanour that would help her through many hardships in the years ahead but, despite this, she was governed by her father's wishes as well as being ruled by her brother Cesare's domineering will power – something that would, at various stages throughout their lives, bring the siblings to an intense dislike of each other, at least on the part of Lucrezia. But despite this, they very much loved each other. Perhaps it was their closeness that helped bring about the rumours of incest. But it cannot be denied that Lucrezia was one of only three women who Cesare ever truly admired, and the only woman he ever really loved.

Regarding Borgia's other children, Juan, who was always seen as Cardinal Borgia's favourite, was described as incredibly spoiled but also incredibly handsome. His vain and overly self-indulgent character would only help him on his way to a sticky end later in life. Of Gioffre Borgia little is known – contemporaries made no remark of the baby of the Borgia family other than the odd passing comment. He would remain in the shadows for the rest of his life, only popping up when he was to be used in Rodrigo Borgia's political chess games.

Whilst it has been generally accepted by the majority of historians that Cesare, Juan, Lucrezia and Gioffre were the illegitimate children of Cardinal Rodrigo Borgia, there are those who argue the contrary. For instance, Peter de Roo comes to the conclusion that the four Borgia children cannot possibly be the children of Rodrigo for numerous reasons. Firstly he argues that the Borgia children were all born in Spain to a Vanozza and Guillen Ramon Lanzol y de Borja whilst Rodrigo was living in Italy, and that she was certainly no mistress of the Cardinal. He then goes on to state that Rodrigo Borgia all but adopted the children after Guillen's death in around 1481.[6] Going forward he then states that as Pope, Alexander VI called many people in his letters 'Beloved Son' or 'Beloved Daughter', and that such titles, when seen in letters towards the children, does not point to his paternity of them. De Roo also uses a number of documents both from the Vatican Archives and archives across Europe to make his argument, coming to the conclusion that many of the documents which show the Borgia children to be Rodrigo's are actually forgeries and thus, utterly worthless. His main argument for this is based on a number of documents pulled from the Osuna archives in Madrid in which the big question is: If these are genuine papal bulls, why are there no records of them within the Vatican archives? A good question indeed but not one that proves that the documents are forgeries. What is interesting, however, is that with certain documents, De Roo notes down a number of discrepancies that may well indeed point to these documents being forgeries. For instance he examines one bull that offers Pedro Luis de Borja a dispensation and then ends up giving him full legitimisation and finds that the seal is missing, the writing violates the style of the Roman chancery, the difference in the spelling of the names de Borja (Spanish) and Borgia (Italian) – although changes in name spelling were common at the time – and that there are no other examples, especially within the Vatican archives, of dispensations ending in legitimisations.[7] He uses many of these arguments throughout his work, often coming back to the differences in the spelling of the Borgia name. He argues, for instance in his examination of a document relating to Juan (Giovanni) Borgia, that the Spanish spelling of the name – de Borja – would not have been known in Rome at the time so it must have been forged away from Rome by a Spaniard.[8] This is a rather spurious argument to say the least and, in fact, De Roo shows himself as being incredibly subjective throughout his work. Every time he mentions something that contradicts his argument, he calls it 'silly' or the work of 'stupid archslanderers'.[9] The bias in de Roo's work is clear, and it may well stem from the fact the he was a Catholic priest perhaps looking to whitewash and completely clear the name of the Borgia Pope.

G.J. Meyer expands on De Roo's arguments although spends much less time going over the documents, rather spending just a few pages on De Roo's works. Both mention that the Borgia siblings were what are known as 'siblings-German', or siblings who have the same father and mother. They then state that older Borgia siblings such as Pedro Luis de Borja and Girolama were also born of the same parentage rather than by unknown women, which is generally accepted in the Borgia mythos.[10] But if this were the case, then why are only the names of Cesare, Juan, Lucrezia and Gioffre recorded on Vanozza Cattanei's gravestone? As Mallett points out, it seems unlikely that if Vanozza was indeed their mother then they would not have been forgotten – Isabella was still alive at the point of Vanozza's death, after all, and Pedro Luis was the first Duke of Gandia, which was a position of some importance and would have taken precedence over Juan's name on the epitaph.[11] It seems therefore somewhat hasty to attribute the parentage of the Borgia siblings to someone else on such flimsy and subjective evidence, although it is important to realise that there are questions surrounding their paternity.

The careers of the Borgia children were decided and laid out before them even before they could walk. Juan was chosen as the son who would be the military leader, the great Duke who would go on to continue the Borgia line; Cesare was destined for a life in the Church; Lucrezia would be forced into diplomatic marriages and Gioffre would do the same. The children were their father's pawns, important chess pieces but Cesare in particular did not like the career path that was chosen for him.

When Cesare was just six years old, the Pope granted a dispensation that allowed him to hold Church benefices despite his illegitimacy and the following year, 1482, King Ferdinand of Aragon exempted him from a law that would stop him from holding lordships in Spain due to his illegitimacy. Being bastard born would not get in the way of raising Cesare Borgia to the heights that his father so wanted for him.

By the age of just fifteen, Cesare had already been given a vast number of Church benefices including the Bishopric of Pamplona, the ancient capital of Navarre. This caused particular outrage as the young man had not yet taken his holy orders and Cardinal Rodrigo Borgia did his best to calm down the populace, telling them that Cesare's elevation was simply down to his merits and hard work. Cesare, on a break from the University of Perugia and busy on a hunting trip, found himself having to write a letter to the people of Navarre to try and soothe their anger. But it didn't work and the Pope had to intervene to halt the rebellion.

Cesare had begun his university education at Perugia in 1489 and whilst there began to make contact with those who would stay by his side during his later years. Perugia itself was mainly under the control of the Baglioni family despite the government officially being in the hands of papal officials and city magistrates, and the leader of the unruly family was Gian Paolo. Cesare's time in Perugia opened his eyes to just how such cities within Italy worked – the Church may have had official control, but the real control was in the hands of the families who ruled the streets. It was a pattern that he would come across multiple times throughout his life, particularly on the streets of Rome which were dominated by warring and incredibly powerful families. After spending two years at Perugia, Cesare made the move to the University of Pisa in 1491 and there he studied for his doctorate in Canon Law. The university was a highly regarded law school but that was not the only reason for Rodrigo to send his son there – Pisa was controlled by the powerful Medici family and Rodrigo Borgia wanted to make sure that he was on the best terms possible with a family whose patriarch held the sobriquet of 'Il Magnifico'. And so he sent Cesare to be under the protection of Lorenzo the Magnificent, whose own son, Giovanni de' Medici, was also to attend the University of Pisa and was also destined for a career in the Church.

Cesare arrived in Pisa with a huge Spanish household and lived as if he were king of his own court. Such ostentatious display cannot have sat well with Giovanni de' Medici. Although the two young men would have seen a lot of each other, Giovanni's true reaction to the Bishop of Pamplona must have involved a rather bitter taste being left in his mouth. Indeed, Giovanni's chancellor commented on the poor behaviour of Cesare and his household.[12] But despite this, Cesare was noted as an exceptional scholar with an 'ardent mind'.[13]

In 1492 events were about to shake Italy, and the world of the Borgia family, to their core. Young Giovanni de' Medici was accepted into the College of Cardinals and on his way to Rome he stopped off in Florence to see his ailing father. Before he left, Lorenzo wrote a letter to his son warning him to be careful as he was about to enter a 'sink of all iniquities'.[14] It was a mixture of instructions as to how his son could lead a pious life as well as a warning to watch out for the corruption that existed within the walls of the Vatican. And with the benefit of hindsight, given what would happen in the months following the writing of this letter, it can perhaps be seen as a warning about the corruption of the next Pope – Rodrigo Borgia.

'Your promotion to the Cardinalate, as you may imagine, at your age and for the other reasons already mentioned, will be viewed with great envy, and those who were not able to prevent your attaining this dignity will endeavour, little by little, to diminish it by lowering you in public estimation and causing you to slide into the same ditch into which they have themselves fallen, counting on success because of your youth. You must be all the firmer in your stand against these difficulties, as at present one sees such lack of virtue in the college.'[15]

Just a month later, Lorenzo the Magnificent died at his villa in Careggi with his dear friends Angelo Poliziano and Giovanni Pico della Mirandola at his side. The Dominican friar Girolamo Savonarola had visited him at his bedside at the behest of Lorenzo himself. Whilst the exact nature of his illness is unknown, it cannot be denied that by the time of his death Lorenzo was in a huge amount of pain. During the visit from Savonarola, it is said that the friar refused to listen to Lorenzo's final confession, advising the dying man that before he would hear the confession, he demanded three things that had to be acceded to. Whilst Lorenzo acceded to the first two, he refused to accede to the last and so the friar left without listening to Lorenzo's final confession. There are other accounts of the visit, however, which seem far more plausible than the three demands that have become ingrained in the legend surrounding Lorenzo the Magnificent. Angelo Poliziano wrote about the visit just weeks after Lorenzo's death, stating that Lorenzo simply advised Savonarola that he remained firm in his religious faith.[16]

Just a few months later, Pope Innocent VIII died. Innocent had been Pope for eight years and had succeeded Sixtus IV in a papal Conclave that had been Rodrigo Borgia's first real attempt at winning the Papal tiara. Innocent, who had been named Giovanni Battista Cibo before his election, had been a compromise in the Conclave after a stalemate between Borgia and his main rival Giuliano della Roverre. Roverre, realising that he would not be able to gain the majority vote required, quickly worked at having one of his own elected to the Papacy. When Innocent took the chair of St Peter in 1484, Giuliano della Roverre was the one who really held the reins of power. But by 1492 it became clear that Innocent was on his deathbed and, despite the work of physicians to try and help, there was nothing that could be done. Innocent was given human milk to try and nourish him. Another story, completely unsubstantiated, is that Innocent was seen by a Jewish doctor who prescribed the blood of young Jewish boys which could save the Pope's life. The boys perished due to the bloodletting, and Pope Innocent VIII was not saved. Rather, the doctor fled and a warrant was issued for his arrest.[17]

Pope Innocent breathed his last on 25 July 1492 and in his final days had witnessed a huge breaking down of relations between Cardinal Borgia and Cardinal della Roverre. The two men had fought at the Pope's bedside and quarrelled over who would be given the keys to the Castel Sant' Angelo. The two men had never gotten on and had gone head to head in previous Papal elections. It was about to happen again and on 6 August 1492, Cardinal Rodrigo Borgia entered the Conclave with twenty four of his fellow Cardinals.

When he exited the Conclave, it would be as Pope. And the world of Cesare and Lucrezia Borgia was about to be turned on its head.

Chapter 3

The Papal Conclave

Following the death of Pope Innocent VIII in July 1492, and before the College of Cardinals met to elect the new Pope, preparations had to be made. These preparations were left entirely to the Papal Master of Ceremonies, Johannes Burchard, who recorded everything diligently in his diaries – each Cardinal had to be provided with a number of items to see him through the trials of the Conclave:

'A tabula or table, five palms in length, with its supports, a chair, a stool, a seat for the dischargements of the stomach with its appurtenances. Two urinals, a cabasium. Two small napkins for the table of the Lord. Twelve little table napkins for the same Lord. Four hand towels. A cape for the members of the Conclave. Two little cloths for wiping cups. Capel. A chest or box for the garments of the Lord, his shirts, rochets, towels for wiping the face and handkerchiefs. One mantle for assisting at the ceremonies with its hood. Four boxes of sweets as a provision. One vessel of sugared pine seeds. Marzipan. Cane sugar. Biscuits. A lump of sugar. A small pair of scales. A hammer. Keys. A spit. A needle case. A writing case with penknife, forceps, pens, reed pens and pen stand. A quire of paper for writing. Red wax. A water jug. A water jug containing holy water. Six cups. Six vessels. A salt cellar. Knives for cutting. Little knives for the table of the Lord....'[1]

Such organisation was truly Burchard's forte and he made sure that everything was followed to the letter. After all, the Cardinals would be locked in seclusion until they elected a new Pontiff so everything had to be perfect. Yet despite the tight organisation and regulation, corruption still went on within the walls of the Vatican during the Conclave. And it is this corruption, vote buying and simony, that got Rodrigo Borgia elected as Pope Alexander VI.

When the Cardinals entered the Conclave and were locked inside, they were already split into two main factions – one followed Giuliano della Roverre, nephew of the late Pope Sixtus IV and preferred choice of the king of France as well as Naples, whilst the other sat behind Ascanio Sforza, Milan's choice for the Papacy. The split, however, meant that there would be a deadlock and so the wheeling and dealing began in earnest. Before the Conclave had even begun, it was widely believed that the French king had transferred 200,000 ducats to Rome in order to ensure della Roverre's election as Pope, although it became obvious very quickly that he had no chance of becoming Pope, at least in this election. Not only that, but French interference in the Conclave just wasn't welcome.

During the first week of voting, no Cardinal came out with any sort of majority in the votes and this is where Rodrigo Borgia's astute political mind, and his willingness to bribe, came into play. Borgia, who had been Papal Vice Chancellor and served under five different Popes, is said to have used his huge amount of wealth to buy the votes that would elect him. But up until the last, he found himself pitted against Ascanio Sforza and those who supported him. A private conversation between the two ensued in which Sforza was offered not only the post of Vice Chancellor but cash as well – the story goes that mules carrying cases of cash were sent to Sforza's palace in payment for his vote.[2] This seems to be invention on the part of Infessura, a biographer and diarist who was extremely anti-Papal. We can gauge the fact that this is entirely made up due to Infessura stating that Borgia gave Cardinal Orsini his house as a reward – the house was actually given to Sforza, thus proving Infessura's ignorance of the event.[3] Rodrigo also gave away many of his benefices – however, every newly elected Pope had such things to give away so would the giving away of his benefices count as simony? Either way, the castles of Soriano and Castellana, as well as the Abbey of Subiaco, were given to Cardinals Orsini, Colonna and Savelli.[4] Many who believe in the Borgia myth state that such things were given as a reward for votes, however the more likely explanation is that these benefices were given to the three biggest Roman families as a way of keeping the peace.

The Borgia myth states that simony, bribery and corruption played a huge part in Rodrigo Borgia's election as Pope. But how true is this? It must be noted that after his election, Rodrigo Borgia rewarded every single Cardinal and even those who were hostile towards him received something – Giuliano della Roverre, for instance, was given many favours including the Abbey at Rioux, a pension of 50 ducats a year, canonries and Rectorships. Rodrigo Borgia left no one out, even providing for those Cardinals who were unable to make the election.

By the fourth day of the election, Rodrigo Borgia was just one vote away from winning the throne of St Peter. He had bribed those he could and those he couldn't still refused to vote his way. His last hope lay in the 96 year old Cardinal Maffeo Gherardo. Borgia managed to convince the elderly Venetian and on the fifth day of the Conclave, the Cardinals made their final vote. And as, on 11 August 1492, Rodrigo Borgia's name was announced as having the majority vote, the Spanish Cardinal exclaimed, 'I am Pope!'

Rodrigo took the name Alexander and was proclaimed as Alexander VI. The Papal Master of Ceremonies, Johannes Burchard, was instructed to write the new Pope's name upon slips of paper and scatter them to the crowd thronged outside St Peter's. The name of Alexander VI, the one time Cardinal Borgia would thus be on everyone's lips.

Almost immediately, the people of Rome and beyond began to talk about how Rodrigo Borgia had bought the election, though he was generally greeted favourably. He threw himself into his new role as Pope with gusto and fervour – however some greeted his election with disdain and were unhappy at having a Catalan Pope on the throne of St Peter. Alexander, Rodrigo Borgia, had lived in Rome for many years and was generally a popular figure within the city despite his Catalan heritage.

Still, he made sure that the population of Rome loved him and he did that by reminding them of his ostentation and loved of throwing a good party. His coronation procession was magnificent if somewhat marred by the intense August heat – Alexander fainted no less than three times. The processional route was lined with triumphal arches proclaiming that Pope Alexander VI was God like, whilst all throughout Rome, images of the Borgia Bull popped up, naked youths acted as dancing sculptures and flowers were thrown from houses that lined the route.[5] This magnificent ceremony not only showed the people of Rome how powerful the Borgia family were, but it was also a flamboyant show of just how the Renaissance Papacy worked.

Now, with Alexander VI occupying St Peter's chair, the Borgias were the most powerful family not only in Italy, but across the Christian world. Alexander's children were his way of securing a Borgia dynasty, a dynasty which would hold on to their power and make the family one of the greatest and, in hindsight, notorious, that the world had ever seen.

Chapter 4

The Cardinal and the Duchess

Upon his election to the Papacy, Alexander VI made a number of promises including one which every Pontiff since time immemorial had made – that he would reform the Church. Whether or not the reform would actually come to pass was another matter entirely, but what mattered was that he began his reign with all kinds of good intentions. In a letter to Florence just a few days after the election, Manfredo Manfredi, the Florentine Ambassador, wrote of Alexander's promises to dismiss any tyrannical officials from office and also that he would keep his children away from the Eternal City.[1] And Alexander kept this promise, at least to begin with. Cesare was kept at the castle of Spoleto, where he had remained since his return from Pisa and Lucrezia remained in the household of Adriana de Mila. Despite being kept away from Alexander, the Borgia children were not forgotten. Cesare was quickly granted the Archbishopric of Valencia, along with 16,000 ducats a year and marriage prospects were quickly spoken about for Lucrezia. Juan Borgia was to later be given the position as Gonfalonier – a military and political office in which the chosen individual would head the Papal armies – of the Church. Other members of the Borgia family were also honoured by the newly elected Pope – one of his Lanzol kinsmen was raised to the rank of Cardinal at the very same consistory in which Alexander handed out benefices, and in which he gave the Archbishopric of Valencia to Cesare. Another Lanzol kinsman from Spain, Rodrigo Lanzol y de Borja, was given the captaincy of the Papal Guard.[2]

Rodrigo then made an effort to crack down on other issues that had been affecting Rome since even before the death of his predecessor, Innocent VIII. The numbers are shocking – from the moment that it became known that Innocent was on his death bed, control broke down within the city of Rome with well over 200 murders being committed within the city walls, between the announcement that Innocent was dying and the election of Alexander VI.[3] On 3 September 1492, he had two murderers – the del Rosso brothers – hanged and their house levelled. Other criminals found themselves locked in the cramped and dark dungeons deep within the Castel Sant' Angelo. Not only that, but Alexander issued decrees against corruption and bribery, even setting aside one day a week to hear complaints or petitions from the Roman people. Such actions were remarkable and far ahead of their time and even Infessura, who makes no secret of his extreme dislike and bias towards Alexander, admits that Alexander's reign 'began in a wonderful manner'.[4]

Within just a few months of Alexander's election to the Papacy, the Borgia family were once more together in Rome. Cesare took up residence in a palace within the Borgo, a neighbourhood around the Vatican, where the envoy Boccaccio paid a visit to him. In March 1493, Boccaccio sent a letter back to his master Ercole d'Este in Ferrara, describing the young Archbishop:

> 'On the day before yesterday I found Cesare at home in Trastevere. He was on the point of setting out to go hunting, and entirely in secular habit; that is to say dressed in silk and armed…He is a man of great talent and of an excellent nature; his manners are those of the son of a great prince; above everything, he is joyous and light hearted. He is very modest, much superior to, and of a much finer appearance than his brother the Duke of Gandia, who also is not short of natural gifts. The archbishop never had any inclination for the priesthood…'[5]

It is interesting to note the comparisons in Boccaccio's letter between Cesare and his brother, Juan. We can gauge from the letter than although Cesare is aware of his change in status, he has not allowed it to go to his head. Juan however, seems to have done completely the opposite. He was the favourite son and, during these early years of Alexander's Papacy, occupied centre stage far more often than Cesare did. Indeed, the young Duke of Gandia seemed to rather enjoy dressing up in Turkish clothing and going on jaunts with Prince Djem, a prisoner of the Vatican since he had been defeated by his brother Sultan Bazajet in a war of succession. Djem had been a prisoner since 1489, with a decent sized bribe of 40,000 ducats per year to keep him locked up in comfort.[6]

Lucrezia, at this time, lived in the palace of Santa Maria in Portico and was kept well away from her mother's household. The palace was also lived in by Alexander's cousin, as Lucrezia's carer, Adriana de Mila. Giulia Farnese, Adriana's daughter in law and Alexander's mistress, also occupied the palace.

As has been previously mentioned, all of Alexander's children had their lives and careers planned out for them. Whilst Cesare was to be made a Cardinal and Juan was to be Gonfalonier of the Papal army, Lucrezia was to be used in alliances for the family through marriage. Now that Alexander occupied the chair of St Peter, this became all the more important and on 2 February 1493, Lucrezia Borgia was betrothed to Giovanni Sforza, the Lord of Pesaro and relation to both Cardinal Ascanio Sforza and the powerful Ludovico 'Il Moro' Sforza of Milan. Such a match was, of course, a political one – Milan was a huge power in Italian politics, yet the relations between Milan and the other big power, Naples, was on the verge of collapsing completely. Il Moro wanted to take the Dukedom of Milan from his nephew, Gian Galeazzo Sforza, whose wife, Isabella d' Aragona, disliked how he was leaving day to day business to his uncle, and so wrote scathing letters to her grandfather in Naples, complaining that it was obvious Ludovico wanted the Dukedom for himself. Both parties wanted the Pope on their side, very much in the same way as France and Spain did. Both of these foreign powers also had claims to the throne of Naples which was currently being held by King Ferdinand of Spain's own family. Ludovico Sforza thus wanted Ferrante of Naples out of the picture and so invited the French king, who had a claim to Naples himself, to invade Italy and take the important southern city. Such complicated politics lay at the backdrop to Lucrezia's wedding to Giovanni Sforza as well as a wish on Alexander's part to show his gratitude for Ascanio Sforza's help in securing his Papacy.

The wedding took place on 12 June 1493, although the two had previously been married by proxy on 2 February. Lucrezia brought with her a dowry of 30,000 ducats. The wedding itself was a magnificent affair, full of the pomp and circumstance that came to be associated with the Borgia family. Just two days previously, Sforza made a magnificent entry into Rome and stopped outside Santa Maria in Portico so his young bride to be could have her first glimpse of him. She was, at this stage, just 13 years old so her new husband – aged 26 – must have seemed ancient to her. Such a prospect must have been incredibly frightening.

The wedding was attended by some of the most prominent members of society, during which the couple were presented with magnificent gifts. Boccaccio describes the wedding in a letter to his master, mentioning the grand gifts that were presented to the new couple – the Duke of Milan presented the couple with a gift of gold brocade, two rings, a diamond and a ruby. Ascanio Sforza gave a silver drinking service, Cardinal Monreale gave two rings of sapphire and diamond, Cesarini gave the couple a bowl and cup, Juan Borgia gave a drinking vessel – and the gifts just kept on coming.[7] Following the ceremony, Pope Alexander held a private dinner which was attended by people such as Juan, Duke of Gandia, Cardinal Ascanio Sforza and Cardinal Sanseverino. Traditionally, at the end of the night there would be a bedding ceremony in which the marriage would have been consummated; however, on this occasion, the ceremony did not happen. Pope Alexander ordered that the marriage was not to be consummated until the November, possibly out of concern for his daughter's young age but it was more than likely a way of keeping the door open for dissolution of the marriage on the grounds of non-consummation. The whole marriage was, of course, part of Alexander's complicated political chess game.

With Lucrezia now tied to the Sforza family, Pope Alexander could concentrate on cementing other political alliances. Set against the backdrop of the issue of Naples, just eight days after Lucrezia's wedding, the Spanish envoy arrived in Rome and informed the Pope that King Ferdinand considered the Aragonese cause in Naples as his own – after all, they were family – and the two powerful heads of state entered into another round of intense negotiations. Ferdinand wanted Naples and he also wanted sovereignty over the New World that had been discovered by Christopher Columbus – in return he would give his cousin, Maria Enriquez, in marriage to the Pope's son Juan. To back the offer up, King Ferrante of Naples offered his bastard daughter Sancia's hand in marriage to Gioffre. Alexander, hungry to establish his family as a powerful dynasty, hastily agreed to these terms and a marriage was swiftly arranged between Juan and Maria Enriquez. Juan left for Spain in August 1493 and just two weeks later, Gioffre was married by proxy to Sancia of Aragon. The boy had been quickly legitimised by Pope Alexander in order for the marriage to happen.[8]

With the marriages of his other children now dealt with, Alexander could now concentrate on his plans for Cesare. The young Archbishop of Valencia's career was to take him into the college of Cardinals however there was a big problem – he was illegitimate, and if he was to be a Cardinal then that problem would have to be quickly removed. A papal bull was issued on 20 September 1493 declaring that Cesare was the legitimate son of Vanozza Cattanei and her husband, Domenico da Rignano whilst a second, secret bull was issued on the same day saying that Cesare was actually the son of Pope Alexander VI. De Roo, as we have already discussed previously, demarks this secret bull as a forgery based on a number of points – all of which are incredibly subjective – including that it is 'morally impossible that a Pope would, without any need, by mere incident as it were, not only shamelessly admit, but boastingly describe his own heinous immorality…Alexander VI was not so demented to allow himself such a public bravado'.[9] With these bulls now in place, the Cardinals who had been charged with the examining of Cesare's birth status, Pallavicini and Orsini, had to conclude that Cesare was indeed of legitimate birth and that he could be admitted into the College of Cardinals.

It was to be expected that Cesare's admission into the consistory would cause an absolute uproar. Cardinal Giuliano della Roverre, ever one for the dramatic, was so angry over it that he took to his bed with a fever. But although Cesare was young, at just eighteen years old and having not yet taken Holy orders, his elevation to the Cardinalate was no less scandalous than the elevation of Ippolito d'Este, who was just fifteen years old, and Alessandro Farnese, the brother of Alexander's mistress Giulia. Despite these appointments, Alexander also raised older men of worth including John Morton, Archbishop of Canterbury, as well as two Frenchman and a Venetian. The proposed list of new Cardinals was put forward on 18 September 1493 and caused such an uproar that Alexander completely lost his temper with the consistory, threatening that he would show them just what sort of a Pope he was by making more Cardinals they did not like by Christmas if they did not bow to his demands in this. Still, the list of promoted Cardinals were only passed after an incredibly close vote on 20 September. The new Cardinals were voted in by the skin of their teeth, with ten Cardinals opposing and just eleven agreeing with Pope Alexander. The news was greeted with jubilation, especially by the Farnese family, for it meant that not only was Giulia in the pontiff's bed but there was now also a Farnese in the College of Cardinals. Indeed, Giulia's sister wrote to her husband Puccio in jubilation over the fact that it was now even more likely for other members of the family to be granted papal favours:

'You will have received letters from Florence before mine reaches you and have learned what benefices have fallen to Lorenzo, and all that Giulia has secured for him, and you will be greatly pleased.'[10]

The name Lorenzo refers to Lorenzo Pucci, who later rose to prominence under Pope Leo X.

Cesare was away from Rome, in Caprarola, when he received the news that he had been voted into the College of Cardinals. The young man was spending time away from the summer heat and plague that ravaged the city during the hot months and had been spending his time writing argumentative letters about the result of the Il Palio horse race rather than concentrating on his Church duties. The race in question had taken place on 16 August and had been won by the jockey riding Cesare's horse, who used a technique that can only be described as cheating in order to win – he threw himself off the horse at the most perfect moment, thus making the horse lighter and enabling it to cross the finish line first. Francesco Gonzaga, the Marquess of Mantua, put in a complaint when his horse came second because of this blatant bit of cheating – the judges of the Il Palio upheld the complaint and Cesare, who despised being beaten, sat down to write a series of letters to the governors of Siena, where the race was held. We do not know what the outcome of this row was, however we can be sure that Cesare warned the governors of Siena that it would be better for them to have him as an ally rather than the Marquess of Mantua:

'Have respect to our honour, commanding that the Palio should be given to us, in which you will give us singular pleasure and we will remain obligated to do things which will be to the pleasure and honour of your Magnificent persons and most noble commune.'[11]

Already, Cesare Borgia was exhibiting the sort of behaviour that would set him above the rest in his later life and career away from the Church.

Cesare returned to Rome on 17 October in order to take up his position of Cardinal of Valencia as well as councillor to his father, the Pope. Not long after Cesare's elevation to the Cardinalate, news reached Rome of the poor behaviour of Juan, who had previously travelled to Spain in order to marry Maria-Enriquez – there were reports that he had not consummated his marriage with his wife, that Ferdinand and Isabella had not attended the wedding, that Juan spent his time killing cats and dogs for fun and that he spent more time in brothels than with his wife. Cesare, the new Cardinal of Valencia, sat down to write his wayward brother a letter demanding that he rein his behaviour in:

> 'However great my joy and happiness at being promoted Cardinal, and they were certainly considerable, my annoyance was greater still when I heard of the bad reports His Holiness had received of you and your behaviour. Letters…have informed His Holiness that you have been going round Barcelona at night, killing cats and dogs, making frequent visits to the brothel, gambling for large sums, speaking disrespectfully and imprudently to important people, showing disobedience to Don Erich and Donna Maria and finally acting throughout in a way inconsistent with a gentleman of your position.'[12]

That summer, as every summer before it, plague had raged throughout Rome. Lucrezia's new husband, Giovanni Sforza, had taken himself away from Rome during the August of 1493 and gone to Civita Castellana. There is no record of Lucrezia leaving Rome to be with her husband. She was certainly in the Eternal City by the October of that year along with Sforza, where it seems he was given permission to sleep with his wife who was still only thirteen years old. Sforza himself made use of the fact that his young wife was one of the best ways to become close with the Holy Father – he even boasted about such access to the Mantuan envoy and said that 'all these women that surround the pontiff' were worth speaking to, but 'principally his wife'.[13] He was right, of course. The best way to curry favour with Alexander VI was through the women who were in residence at the palace of Santa Maria in Portico – his mistress, Giulia Farnese, his cousin Adriana de Mila and his daughter, the Duchess of Pesaro. Presents were one of the best ways to gain access to the Pontiff through these women – gifts of food were often given, as were beautiful jewels.

But the political situation in Italy was once more becoming dangerous and it was a situation that would have dire consequences for the Sforza-

Borgia alliance, even if Giovanni Sforza himself did not yet realise it. The situation was a precarious one – in the January of 1494, King Ferrante of Naples had died and in the March of that year, Alexander VI had announced his intentions that he would support Ferrante's son Alfonso in his claim to the throne and have him crowned king. Such a decision not only meant that the French, whose own king had a claim to the throne of Naples, would more than likely invade Italy with the aim of taking Naples by force, but also that it put the Sforzas in a very awkward situation indeed. After all Naples and Milan were enemies, so how could they sit idly by and support the Pope's decision to ally himself with Naples?

Giovanni knew his position was a precarious one – he had to be seen to support the family he had married into but he also had to support his own family. He was called before the Pope in the April of 1494, who was somewhat irritated with Sforza's dithering – Giovanni wrote of the meeting in a letter to his patron, Ludovico:

'Yesterday his Holiness said to me in the presence of Monsignor (Cardinal Ascanio), "Well, Giovanni Sforza! What have you to say to me?" I answered, "Holy Father, every one in Rome believes that your Holiness has entered into an agreement with the King of Naples, who is an enemy of the state of Milan. If this is so, I am in an awkward position, as I am in the pay of your Holiness and also in that of the state I have named. If things continue as they are, I do not know how I can serve one party without falling out with the other, and at the same time I do not wish to offend. I ask that your Holiness may be pleased to define my position so that I may not become an enemy of my own blood, and not act contrary to the obligations into which I have entered by virtue of my agreement with your Holiness and the illustrious State of Milan." He replied, saying that I took too much interest in his affairs, and that I should choose in whose pay I would remain according to my contract. And then he commanded the above named monsignor to write to your Excellency what you will learn from his lordship's letter.

My Lord, if I had foreseen in what a position I was to be placed I would sooner have eaten the straw under my body than have entered into such an agreement. I cast myself into your arms. I beg your Excellency not to desert me, but to give me help, favour and advice how to resolve the difficulty in which I am placed, so that I may remain a good servant of Your Excellency. Preserve for me the position and the little nest which, thanks to the mercy of Milan, my ancestors left me, and I and my men of war will ever remain at the service of your Excellency.'[14]

Pope Alexander replied that Giovanni Sforza should choose whose side he was on, whilst Sforza himself tried desperately to keep both sides happy. He wrote to Juan Borgia, with whom he got on very well, and mentioned that he would soon be leaving for Pesaro, and Lucrezia would be going with him. He even mentioned, as if to butter Juan up a little, that he would be looking to get hold of the horses Juan wanted from the King of Naples. It didn't help, however. Alexander's allegiance to Naples was made concrete with the marriage between Gioffre and Sancia, the alliance also bringing with it a number of titles for Juan.

Despite his dithering, Giovanni Sforza was just about hanging on to favour with his wife's family. In May 1494, Pope Alexander finally granted Sforza permission to leave Rome for Pesaro and he allowed Lucrezia to accompany him, along with Adriana de Mila and Giulia Farnese. They arrived in Pesaro in June in the midst of an incredibly heavy rain storm. Yet despite the rain, the people of Pesaro came out to enthusiastically greet their new Duchess. The visit to Pesaro came at a dangerous time for Rome and, from the safety of the little town, Lucrezia was told of the ills happening in Rome in a dispatch from Francesco Gacet, a confidant of Alexander. He reported that not only was the plague once more sweeping the Eternal City, but Alexander was also beset by pro-French factions there – mainly the troublesome Colonna family. Lucrezia wrote to her father, asking him to take the greatest care of himself during such a difficult time. But despite the difficulties at home, Lucrezia and her ladies made the most of their stay in Pesaro. They dressed beautifully and danced together, bewitching the court of Pesaro with their beauty.

Alexander soon became desperate to have the women back in Rome, writing to them and asking when they would return. Although they were expected back in the city by June, Lucrezia was having too much of a good time to even think about returning, let alone write to her father regularly. Alexander, who adored his daughter and who was completely obsessed with his mistress, began to panic and by the end of June had convinced himself that the women in Pesaro had died, or were so ill that they would not live – it was only when he received a letter written by his daughter that he calmed down, realising that the rumours flying around more were nothing more than that. But Alexander's fury could not be abated when he found out that, despite asking and ordering her back to Rome, Giulia Farnese had left Pesaro for the Farnese estate of Capodimonte in July, in order to visit her sick brother. So obsessed was he, so worried for her safety with the imminent French invasion, that he wrote a scathing and furious letter to his daughter who remained in Pesaro:

> 'Truly, Lord Giovanni and yourself have displayed little thought for me in this departure of Madonna Adriana and Giulia: for you should have remembered…that such a departure without our knowledge would cause us the greatest displeasure.'[15]

When Giulia reached Capodimonte, she found her brother dead. The grief caused her and her brother, Cardinal Alessandro Farnese, to fall sick and Alexander sent his doctors to treat them. Despite this, as well as sweet words from Alexander stating he was the one who loved her most in the world, Giulia was reluctant to return to Rome and stated she could not do such a thing without her husband's permission. Alexander once more grew furious with Giulia, demanding that she return to Rome forthwith – she remained stubborn and envoys were sent back and forth from Capodimonte to Rome whilst Alexander grew positively apoplectic, writing to her stating that she wanted to join her husband in Basanello for the sole purpose of 'surrendering yourself to that stallion'. Alexander even went as far as threatening both Giulia and Adriana with excommunication if they did not return to Rome. The two women left for Rome and, just a short while down the road, were captured by a group of French soldiers who were led by Yves de Allegre. Although the two women were treated well, Alexander was frantic with worry and immediately agreed to the ransom of 3,000 ducats. Both women were freed and were met by Alexander, who had dressed himself up in military like gear to meet them.

The French arrived in Italy in 1494, headed by the French king, Charles VIII. His coming had been prophesised in Florence by Savonarola, who hailed his coming as that of a 'New Cyrus' – this was a direct comparison to Cyrus the Great, who founded the Achaemenian empire in Persia and conquered vast amounts of land that had belonged to the most powerful empires of his day. On 17 March 1494, Charles VIII had announced his intention to invade Italy in order to take Naples, a city which was considered to be French soil as it belonged to Charles's cousin Louis, Duc d'Orleans. When Charles crossed the Alps, it was with the largest army that had been seen in Europe for well over a century – the total French force was made up of 1,900 lances, 1,200 mounted archers and 19,000 infantry. These were to be supported by 1,500 Italian lances and 2–3,000 Italian infantry.[16] The Italians, impressed with the size of his army as well as his impressive artillery, flocked to see him as he made his way through the country. Whilst at Asti, Charles suffered with a bout of smallpox and took time to recover, however as soon as he was well, he carried on, stopping at Pavia to visit the unwell Gian Galeazzo Sforza, whose wife tried desperately to gain the help of Charles in defending the rights of her husband. However, her pleas fell on deaf ears – ten days later he was dead, poisoned, it was said, by his uncle Ludovico Sforza who had coveted the title of Duke of Milan. When the army reached Florence, Piero de' Medici gave the city up without a fight – Savonarola's prophecy, it seemed, had come true.

With Charles in Florence, the people rose up against the Medici and ousted them. Savonarola was now ruler of the city in all but name, governing the populace from his pulpit. And whilst Charles was in Florence, he demanded free passage through the Papal States – Alexander VI and his family were cornered. If he did not give the French king permission, then he threatened the Pope with a General Council. That could mean only one thing – the deposition of Alexander VI. But Alexander refused to capitulate, declaring to the Ferrarese envoys that he would prefer to leave Rome than become a 'slave of the King of France' and that he did not wish to see Rome 'in the hands of anyone but Italians'.[17] Charles continued southwards, through the Papal States and towards Rome – the Colonna family capitulated to the French in the September of 1494, handing Ostia over to Charles. With Ostia now in French hands, it meant that French warships would have control of the Tiber, blocking Rome's access to the sea and thus much of Rome's trade. And as the Colonna also held the road that connected Rome to Naples, they had the Vatican at bay. The wound was only made worse when, on 17 December, the French took Civitavecchia and the Orsini family handed over the fortress of Bracciano.

The French were on Rome's doorstep and the Cardinals began to take flight. The treasures of the Vatican were locked away in the Castel Sant' Angelo and it was planned for the Pope and his family to take refuge in the huge fortress; however, at the last moment Alexander refused to go. He was joined by Ferrandino, Alfonso II of Naples' son, whose army was ready to fight for the Pope. But, after investing Ferrandino with the dukedom of Calabria on Christmas day 1494, Alexander asked that the young man leave. He also opened the doors of the prison, setting free important prisoners such as Ascanio Sforza and Prospero Colonna. He then, finally, decided to take refuge behind the high walls of the Castel Sant' Angelo. But then, on the very same day, he announced that he would admit the French king into the city of Rome.

Charles entered Rome formally on 31 December 1494, and the meeting between Pope and King took place in the first week of January,

1495. During the French occupation of the city, the troops raided the houses of many important people – the houses of both Cesare and his mother were stripped completely bare. Before a meeting between Charles and Alexander even happened, Alexander tried to play the long game. A number of demands were sent to him as he hid behind the walls of the Castel Sant' Angelo – if he wanted to talk to the king, then he would have to give up the Castel, Cesare would have to be made Papal Legate to France – essentially rendering him a hostage – and the Prince Djem, brother of Sultan Bayezid II was to be handed over to Charles. Alexander refused, sitting himself quite happily within the Papal apartments at the Castel. A problem came when a section of the defensive wall collapsed of its own accord – it made Alexander reconsider his position and negotiations began.

Alexander, backed into a corner, was forced to hand over things that he could not deny the king. Charles was given free passage through the Papal States as well as possession of many papal fortresses including Civitavecchia, Viterbo and Spoleto. Prince Djem was also handed over, though Alexander was to keep the 40,000 ducats that Bayezid paid annually to keep Djem from being set free. Alexander also agreed to send his son, Cesare Borgia, with Charles as Papal Legate to France. Or rather, as a hostage.

The two men now seemed to be the best of friends, with Charles even making a public profession of obedience to the Pope. Alexander even called the King his 'first born son'. It seems that the honeymoon period between King and Pope was entirely down to Alexander's cordial personality in such situations. A wily politician, he knew how to get himself in the French king's good graces – Charles even seemed to forget about his wish for reform of the Church and deposing Alexander. Alexander's charms had turned the French king completely about-face.

On 28 January 1495, Charles made to leave Rome with Cesare at his side. Before departing, he met with the Pope at the Palazzo Venezia:

'King and Pope remained closeted together for a short while, and were then joined for a further quarter of an hour by Cardinal

Cesare Borgia, after which His Majesty was escorted by the Pope and Cardinals through the halls as far as the passage leading to the upper apartments of the palace. There the King knelt down bareheaded, and the Pope, removing his biretta kissed him, but refused quite firmly to allow him to smother his feet with kisses, which His Majesty seemed want to do. The King then departed, mounting his horse at the steps of the gate of the private garden, after waiting for a brief period for Cardinal Cesare Borgia to join him.'[18]

Cesare Borgia, a hostage of Charles VIII in all but name, was about to show the world just how wily he could be, a foreshadowing of his future self, his love of dramatic coups and the wearing of disguises.

Following their departure from Rome, the French party camped in the little town of Velletri. But the next morning, the party discovered that Cesare was nowhere to be found – he had slipped away during the night dressed as a stable boy, and travelled so swiftly that he managed to spend the next night in Rome. However, in order to at least try to keep the peace between his father and the French king, Cesare left Rome the very next day and made for the castle of Spoleto. The French King exploded with rage, screaming that 'All Italians are dirty dogs and the Holy Father is the worst of them!'[19] Cesare's escape completely violated the terms that had been agreed between himself and the Pope but when complaints were taken to Alexander, the Pope insisted that he had no idea where his son was. Charles' soldiers, following the flight of the Cardinal of Valencia, fell greedily upon the mules that had been left behind. They had supposed them to be carrying gold and rich baggage, however, the men found that they had been doubly duped. The chests were empty, filled with nothing but stones. Burchard, however, states in his diary:

'His Majesty quite blatantly kept them after the Cardinal's flight, although, so I was told, nothing was found in their boxes. I do not believe this was true'[20]

Cesare kept himself closeted away at Spoleto until the end of March when he returned to Rome to help his father with negotiations that were due to take place for an alliance against France. On 31 March, an agreement was signed between Milan, Venice, Spain, the Holy Roman Empire and the Pope. It became known as the Holy League. Meanwhile, Charles continued his march southwards towards Naples, evidently determined not to let the embarrassment of Cesare's escape stop him from getting what he wanted. He entered Naples on 22 February 1495 and immediately began to immerse himself in the delights of his new kingdom. With the Aragon family having fled to Sicily, there was nothing to stop him from enjoying himself. Charles and his soldiers indulged themselves in the pleasures of the flesh and were blind to the fact that, despite having originally been celebrated when they arrived, the Neapolitan people had become more than a little annoyed with their new French masters. They were far too interested in wine and women. And what was worse, the 'clownish, dirty and dissolute people', as reported by a Venetian ambassador, had brought with them a new disease that very quickly took hold – syphilis. But Charles still remained, despite suffering setback after setback, including the death of his hostage Prince Djem on 25 February, less than a week after arriving in the city. Rumours abounded that Djem must have been poisoned by Alexander VI – happily seeming to forget that Alexander was receiving 40,000 ducats a year for the Prince's upkeep – and that, despite it happening a month after their departure from Rome, the poison administered must be a secret, slow acting recipe only known by the Borgia family.[21]

Charles finally left Naples on 20 May, followed by a huge number of mules laden down with treasure. As Charles and the remainder of his army began to retrace their steps homeward, Alexander and Cesare left Rome for Orvieto on 27 May, accompanied with a large number of Cardinals and papal troops. None of them wanted to be around when Charles found his way back to the Eternal City, least of all Pope Alexander VI. The city was thus empty when Charles arrived four days later. When Charles left Rome, Alexander and Cesare retreated to Perugia. They wanted to be as far away from the French king as was humanly possible. Then, on 5 July, Charles' troops met the forces of the Holy League at Fornovo on the River Taro – the battle was indecisive but Francesco Gonzaga, the leader of the Holy League's forces, claimed victory. Charles also claimed victory – his troops had, after all, decimated the Italians and left 3,500 of them dead. But the Italians had captured a huge amount of Charles's booty – over 300,000 ducats.[22] It was a pyrrhic victory – yet Charles still scarpered back to France with his tail between his legs.

The Borgia family, minus Lucrezia who was still safely ensconced in Pesaro, returned to Rome. They were triumphant and Alexander happily made Cesare the governor of Orvieto, something that was not met happily with by the citizens of the town.

The years of 1494–5 had seen some of Cesare and Lucrezia's first moves on the political chessboard. Whilst Lucrezia's, for the moment, were small, Cesare's were much bigger. With the benefit of hindsight, we can see that these events foreshadowed Cesare's future – he was provided with the first-hand experience of politics that would serve him so well in his later years. And it cannot be denied that these months of war, politics and shows of utter power instilled in the young Borgia an innate fascination that would end up being either his ultimate triumph, or his downfall.

Chapter 5

'The Duke of Gandia is Dead'

Lucrezia was safely tucked away in Pesaro whilst the drama of the French invasion unfolded in Rome and her husband, Giovanni Sforza, dithered about having his wife return to the city. He certainly did not trust the Borgia family and when the Pope sent a letter telling him that in no circumstance was he to return to Rome but rather join the troops of the Holy League, Giovanni ignored the order completely. Rather it seems he was planning to take himself off to Milan where he would beg the protection of Il Moro. He was in Rome in the April of 1496 however, presumably to get as much money for the condotta, or military contract, that he would never take up as he could. He also resisted suggestions that he should leave the city as soon as he could – he ended up staying there for ten days. Already rumours were rife throughout Rome that there was something wrong in the Borgia-Sforza marriage. But what the rumourmongers did not suspect was that the Borgia family were already planning to have the marriage annulled.

Lucrezia returned to the Vatican, to her old palace of Santa Maria in Portico, in the April of 1496 and in May the Borgia family reunion was complete when Gioffre and Sancia returned to Rome. Sancia's reputation had come before her – gorgeously attired for her ostentatious entry to Rome, Lucrezia was anxious not to be outdone. Indeed the Mantuan envoy, Gian Carlo Scalona, wrote of Gioffre and Sancia's homecoming:

'In truth she [Sancia] did not appear as beautiful as she had been made out to be. Indeed the Lady of Pesaro [Lucrezia] surpassed her. However that may be, by her gestures and aspect the sheep will put herself easily at the disposal of the wolf.'[1]

Scalona's prediction was indeed correct. Rumours had already reached Rome of Sancia's poor behaviour and overly sexual nature. But who could blame her? Her husband was far too young – it was said that he had burst into tears on his wedding night – to satisfy her. In fact, not long after her arrival in Rome, she began an affair with Cesare Borgia himself. Despite this, she and Lucrezia became close friends, often causing mischief together. One such example shows the sort of carefree mischief that the two girls caused. On 22 May, during Mass at St Peter's, the two grew bored during an incredibly long sermon. The girls took themselves up to the choir, which was reserved for members of the church, and began to gossip and laugh with their ladies. The congregation was utterly scandalised by such behaviour!

Juan returned to Rome in August, leaving his pregnant wife Maria behind in Spain. Met at the Porta Portese by Cesare, it was immediately clear that the 20 year old Duke of Gandia had not grown out of his adoration for overly flamboyant clothing – in fact he had not grown out of his love for any sort of ostentation. He returned to Rome dressed in a scarlet cap hung with pearls, a brown velvet doublet covered in jewels, black stockings embroidered in gold with the sigil of Gandia and a Turkish mantle of gold brocade. Even his horse was covered in gold and jewels. He was also accompanied on his entrance back to the Eternal City with six squires that included a Moor dressed in gold and crimson velvet, twelve horses and a crowd of dwarves. It was the sort of spectacle that Rome had come to expect from the Borgia family. And back at the Vatican, Pope Alexander VI greeted his son enthusiastically – the favourite had come home. It cannot have been easy for Cesare, who had been his father's right hand man whilst his brother was away – to watch his father suddenly turn all of his attention back to the prodigal son must have inspired a huge amount of envy in the young Cardinal. In fact, just one month after Juan's return to Rome, ambassador Scalona sent a dispatch to Isabella d'Este stating that, 'Every effort is made to conceal that these sons of the Pope are consumed with envy of each other.'[2]

Whether or not Scalona was exaggerating the 'envy' between Cesare and Juan – sibling rivalry is, after all, completely normal – both brothers knew that they had their parts to play in their father's plans. And unfortunately for Cesare, Juan was the centre of Alexander VI's military plans which was precisely why he had been called back from Spain. For Cesare, his father was paving the way for his son to have a grand ecclesiastical career that would likely end in the Papacy.

One of the biggest issues on Alexander's mind during 1497 was not only the careers of his sons and the problem of Lucrezia's marriage, but also the problem of the Roman barons; the Colonna and Orsini families had long been a thorn in Alexander's side. The two families hated each other and often fought – and they controlled lands which the Pope desperately needed to have control of himself, as well as controlling the roads into Rome. These families, as well as hating each other, despised the Pope. The Orsini family in particular utterly hated the Borgia family, so they were a problem and they needed to be brought to heel.

Alexander VI made the decision to attack the Orsini and he decided to have his army headed by two people who he believed would be the best men for the job – unfortunately his decisions would be the wrong ones. Guidobaldo de Montefeltro, Duke of Urbino, was chosen as commander and Juan Borgia, Duke of Gandia, was to be his second in command. Juan was completely inexperienced militarily, whilst Guidolbaldo had not inherited his father's talents as a condottiere – he was cultured and gentle, not exactly the sort of commander that the Papal army needed. Despite this, the two men were invested with a number of titles. On 26 October, they entered St Peter's where Alexander VI gave his son the titles of Captain General of the Church and Gonfalonier of the Papal army. The very next day, the two men marched out of Rome to begin their campaign against the Orsini.

To start with, the campaign was a complete success with ten out of twelve Orsini strongholds falling within just two months. But then everything went horribly wrong, and Juan Borgia would flee from the field of battle in disgrace.

The fortress of Bracciano was held by Bartolomea Orsini, wife of Bartolomeo d'Alviano. Her husband was one of the best and most respected of the Orsinis' captains and his wife was just as formidable. The siege went horribly wrong very quickly – Guidobaldo was wounded very early on and left Juan in command. What was to come next was quite possibly the most embarrassing moment of the young Duke of Gandia's life.

The Orsini decided to send a donkey into the Papal camp at Bracciano with a sign hung about its neck stating 'I am the ambassador of the Duke of Gandia' and a letter shoved up its backside addressed to the Duke. This wasn't the worst of it, however. A relief force was on its way, commanded by Carlo Orsini and Vitelozzo Vitelli. Juan, sensibly, lifted the siege and moved his artillery safely behind the walls of the town of Anguillara. Guidobaldo re-joined Juan and the two led their men to intercept the army. The two sides clashed at Soriano on 24 January 1497 and it was a hard-fought battle. The Orsini won the day, however. Guidobaldo was taken prisoner and Juan, only slightly injured, fled from the battlefield and headed back to Rome. The young man became a laughing stock for fleeing the battle like a coward. For Alexander, it meant that he had to make a humiliating peace with the Orsini.[3] He refused to pay the ransom demanded for Guidobaldo de Montefeltro, however.

It did not seem that Juan's humiliation was absolute – Alexander sent his son off with the Spanish general Gonsalvo de Cordoba to lay siege to Ostia and take it back after Cardinal della Roverre had given the port to the French. The campaign was a success and on their return to Rome, Juan was given precedence in the celebratory parade. It so incensed de Cordoba that the Spanish captain refused the seat that was offered to him on Palm Sunday – the seat was a step lower than Juan's. Alexander had to settle the differences between the two by diplomatically offering de Cordoba a place in the order of the Golden Rose.

Things were not going well within the Borgia-Sforza marriage, either. Giovanni Sforza suddenly disappeared on Easter morning, declaring that he would be going on a pilgrimage about the Churches of Rome. Instead he took hold of a horse and left the city in such a hurry that he reached Pesaro in just twenty four hours.[4] But what made Giovanni flee from Rome, apparently afraid for his life? Gregorovius mentions that chroniclers at the time stated that Cesare had threatened to kill Giovanni on the basis that he was no longer needed in the Borgia scheme.[5] Whether or not this was the case, it is clear that Giovanni Sforza knew that something was wrong. By 4 May 1497, Giovanni's cousin Ludovico, who had been concerned with a possible falling out with the Pope, learned that it was indeed Borgia threats that had caused Giovanni's flight from Rome. Whilst he promised Giovanni that he would not force his return to the Eternal City, Giovanni did request that he step in to have his wife sent back to Pesaro. A messenger was instructed to send the missive, a message that stated if the Pope then demanded both Giovanni and Lucrezia return to Rome, then Giovanni would of course obey. But by the beginning of June, Ludovico had received letters from the Cardinal Ascanio Sforza stating that the Pope had made up his mind – he wanted an annulment of his daughter's marriage. Lucrezia left the Vatican on 4 June and headed for the convent of San Sisto – it is likely that she took herself off to the convent, a pattern that she would repeat time and again throughout her life, in order to escape the tensions that were rife within the walls of the apostolic palace. After all, her father and brother were desperate to have the Sforza alliance ended and would go to any means necessary to have her free of her husband.

Already rumours were rife as to the reasoning behind the divorce proceedings. The Venetian diarist Sanuto states that one reason was that he had not 'consummated the marriage because he was impotent'.[6] Indeed, it was Giovanni's apparent impotence that was used to annul the marriage between him and Lucrezia. Sforza was, understandably, outraged at the suggestion he had been unable to consummate his marriage due to impotence – he argued that he had known his wife an infinite number of times and that the only reason the Pope wanted the marriage annulled was so that he could have his daughter all to himself. A suggestion was made that Giovanni could prove himself to be potent – the matter that his previous wife, Maddalena Gonzaga, had died in childbirth seemed to be conveniently forgotten. It was even suggested that she had been made pregnant by another. In order to prove that he was not impotent, it was suggested that Sforza should sleep with a woman in the presence of a Papal Legare. Giovanni refused, and the arguments went on.

Whilst Lucrezia was still closeted away in San Sisto, tragedy struck the Vatican and shook the Borgia family to its core. Important decisions had been made in the run up to June 1497, one of which centred on the ongoing issue with Naples. Alexander turned his attention on Naples with one thing on his mind – family.

Alexander had decided to throw his support behind the Aragon family and, with Federigo as the new King, he decided to send one of his Cardinals to formally crown the monarch. His choice for legate was no surprise – Cesare was just twenty two at this point and had only been a Cardinal for three years. The decision therefore was complete and utter nepotism, aimed solely towards gaining more power and prestige for the Borgia family. But it was a decision involving Alexander's other son that seriously raised eyebrows and caused even more resentment towards the already disliked Duke of Gandia. Juan was invested with the duchy of Benevento and given the Papal cities of Terracina and Pontecorvo – these cities were ancient fiefdoms of Naples. However, with Federigo in desperate need of the Pope's goodwill, the grumbling of Naples towards this investiture was kept to just that. Juan, therefore, was now Lord of these cities and they would be passed down to his heirs in perpetuity. These appointments made Juan, who had already made a number of enemies through his behaviour, the target of all hostility towards the Borgia family.

On 14 June, Juan Borgia attended a party at his mother's vineyard along with Cesare. The party is believed to have been held in the garden of a palace next to the church of San Pietro in Vincoli – the iconic steps that lead up to the church are rumoured to be the last place that Juan Borgia was seen alive and are now known as the 'Salita dei Borgia'.[7] It is said that a masked man attended the party with Juan, a man who had repeatedly been seen as part of his entourage. Following the party, as they were returning home, Juan left the company of his brother and stated that he had to go somewhere on his own. Such behaviour was normal for Juan Borgia so little was said, other than a warning that the streets of Rome were dangerous at night so he should not go unaccompanied, especially given the amount of enemies that the young man had. But Juan remained firm in his decision. All he would do was send his groom off to fetch his light armour, telling the young groom to meet him in the Piazza Judea. Juan then rode off with the masked man behind him.

Cesare and Cardinal Juan Borgia Lanzol, a nephew of Pope Alexander, – who had accompanied the brothers after the party with Vanozza Cattanei – lingered a while. Both were uneasy at the way the Duke of Gandia had left, more so about the strange masked man. After waiting a while and seeing no sign of Gandia, they returned to the Vatican. The young groom, who had been sent off to gain his master's armour, had been attacked on his way to the Vatican. Here, some of the accounts differ as to what happened to the groom. Scalona, the Mantuan envoy, reported that he was only lightly wounded 'as he was a strong man'[8] and made his way to the piazza to await his master. When Juan did not show up, he returned to the Vatican, thinking that his master would be spending the night with one of his amorous liaisons. Others report that the groom was found mortally wounded and that he died of his wounds the following day.[9]

The next day, when Juan had not returned, Alexander grew worried but consoled himself in the fact that this was normal behaviour for Juan. He was probably still sleeping off the night before, having spent the night in the arms of a woman. But when night fell and he still had not come home, panic gripped the Vatican. Alexander summoned Cesare to him and demanded to know what had happened. He then, gripped with utter panic for his son's whereabouts, ordered that a search of the city be made. As his men scoured the streets, the panic that already gripped the Pope seized the populace. Shops were closed and homes were barricaded, whilst the powerful families of the city armed themselves to the hilt. And then, on the morning of 16 June 1497, a timber dealer,

Giorgio Schiavi, came forward. The dealer, who often unloaded his wood near the hospital of San Girolamo degli Schiavoni and kept watch of the area, reported that:

'while I was guarding my wood, lying in my boat, two men on foot came out of the alley on the left of the Ospedale...They looked cautiously about them to see that no one was passing and... returned the way they had come. Shortly afterwards, two other men came out of that same alley, also looking furtively around them; not seeing anybody, they made a signal to their companions. Then there appeared a rider on a white horse, carrying a body slung across its crupper behind him, the head and arms hanging to one side, the legs to the other...Having reached the point from which refuse is thrown into the river, the horseman turned his horse so that its tail faced the river, then the two men who were standing on either side, taking the body, one by the hands and arms, the other by the feet and legs, flung it with all their strength into the river.'[10]

When Schiavi was asked why he hadn't come forward sooner, he simply shrugged his shoulders and replied, 'In the course of my life, I must have seen more than 100 bodies thrown into the Tiber from that spot, and I never heard of anyone troubling his head about even one of them.'[11]

A search of the river was then ordered, with all fishermen and boatmen of Rome being brought in to help. A number of bodies were brought up until one caught their attention. Not far from the church of Santa Maria del Popolo a body was brought up in the net of a fisherman by the name of Battistino da Taglia. The body was that of a young, well dressed young man with a purse full of ducats hanging upon his belt. The body was covered in stab wounds – nine, in total – that covered his neck, body and legs.

It was Juan Borgia, Duke of Gandia.

The body of the young duke was taken by boat to the imposing Castel Sant' Angelo where it was quickly made ready for burial. Then, at six o clock that very same evening, Juan Borgia was carried to the Borgia family chapel in the small basilica of Santa Maria del Popolo, accompanied by a procession of 120 torches. The Duke of Gandia was interred within the small chapel where his body still remains, although there is no grave marker to tell visitors just where his body is buried or even anything to say that the hapless Duke of Gandia is interred within the small basilica. It is, for all intents and purposes, as if Juan Borgia has been allowed to be forgotten by the passage of time.

Understandably, Alexander was grief stricken when he heard that his beloved son had been murdered. Johannes Burchard, the Papal master of ceremonies, records Alexander's reaction to the news in his diary:

'On learning that the duke was dead and had been thrown like dung into the river, the Pope was deeply moved and shut himself away in a room in grief and anguish of heart, weeping most bitterly. Cardinal Martini of Segovia with some other servants of His Holiness, came to the door of the apartment, and after they had exhorted, questioned and pleaded for many hours, persuaded the Pope to open the door and let them in. From the Wednesday evening until the following Saturday morning, the Pope ate and drank nothing, whilst from Thursday morning to Sunday, he was quiet for no moment of any hour. At last, however, after the exhortations of these friends, His Holiness agreed to begin ending his mourning insofar as he was able, since he understood that otherwise he would bring greater harm and danger to himself through it.'[12]

But who killed Juan Borgia? An investigation was immediately begun and on Monday 19 June 1497, Alexander had recovered enough to call together a consistory in which he formally announced his son's death and absolved a number of suspects in the murder:

'The Duke of Gandia is dead. A greater calamity could not have befallen us, for we bore him unbounded affection. Life has lost its interest for us. Indeed, had we seven papacies we would give them all to recall the Duke to life. It must be that God thus punishes us for our sins, for the Duke has done nothing to deserve so terrible a fate.'[13]

Alexander reeled off a long list of those who he knew to be innocent of the crime: Giovanni Sforza, Ascanio Sforza, Gioffre Borgia, Guidobaldo da Montefeltro and more. Nothing was mentioned of the Orsini family, however.

Interestingly, a little over a week after his death, the search for Juan's killer was completely called off. It was said that Alexander had done this as he had discovered the truth and that he had forgiven the one who had done the deed. Whether or not that was the case, the people of Rome had their own thoughts over who had murdered the young duke. The Sforzas were one of the first families mentioned, despite Alexander saying that he knew they had nothing to do with the whole thing. After all, in the mind-set of the people, Giovanni Sforza must have wanted some sort of revenge over the embarrassment of his and Lucrezia's divorce proceedings. Juan had also taken revenge on a number of Ascanio Sforza's men after they had killed some of his Spanish grooms, by hanging a number of Sforza's own men from the ramparts of the Torre di Nona. Ascanio, so afraid of the suspicion that had attached himself to his name, had even been avoiding attending consistory. After a search of Ascanio's home was made, and after it was duly noted that Giovanni Sforza wasn't even in Rome at the time of the murder, the Sforza name was cleared. Ascanio then proceeded to visit both the Pope and Cesare to discuss Lucrezia's divorce – it was back to business as usual.

The most likely perpetrators of the crime were the Orsini family. After all, Juan had made enemies of them after he had been at the front of the Borgia attack upon their lands and castles. The family had reason for a vendetta against the Borgias based on this alone but other reasons abounded as to why they would want to exact revenge on the Borgia family. Virginio Orsini, who had been held in deepest confinement within the Castel dell'Uovo, had died in mysterious circumstances. The Orsini family believed that he had been poisoned and were quick to lay the blame at the door of Pope Alexander VI. This called for revenge and what better way to get it than by murdering the man who had taken their lands from them and who was the favourite son of the Supreme Pontiff? It killed two birds with one very bloody stone. The most likely explanation is that they used the prospect of an illicit liaison to lure Juan away, perhaps at the hands of the masked man who had been seen constantly in the Duke's presence. Juan had been in love with a beautiful young lady who was the daughter of Count Antonio della Mirandola and, interestingly enough, Juan's horse was found wandering near the aforementioned lady's house. The Orsini name soon became connected with the murder, with the Ferrarese ambassador, Manfredo Manfredi, mentioning to his master that 'the Pope gives signs of blaming the Orsinis for the murder of his son' and a Venetian report mentioning 'The Orsinis for sure caused the death of his son the Duke of Gandia'.[14]

It was only a year later that rumours started to circulate that Cesare had a hand in his brother's death. It was a logical connection to make – after all, the envy between the two brothers was well known and Cesare had made no secret of his wish to be a soldier. Indeed, for many centuries following the event, it has been generally assumed that Cesare was the guilty party – after all, he had much to gain from his brother's death. It must be noted, however, that he gained nothing from the murder of his brother until much later. Interestingly enough, the rumours that started to circulate a year later began in Venice, a city which was full to bursting with allies of the Orsini. Like many rumours surrounding the Borgia family, it took hold. The diarist Gucciardini, who had no love for the Borgia family, twisted the story in his diary in order to pin the deed on Cesare:

'For, having planned from the beginning of his pontificate to turn all temporal grandeur over to the Duke of Gandia, his first born, the Cardinal of Valencia (whose mind was totally disinclined toward the sacerdotal profession and aspired toward the exercise of arms), not being able to tolerate that this position should be held by his brother, and furthermore envious that Gandia occupied a greater place than himself in the love of Madonna Lucrezia, their common sister, enflamed with lust and ambition (mighty ministers to every great wickedness) one night while his brother was riding alone through Rome, had him killed and cast into the Tiber.'[15]

Gucciardini's argument rests solely on Cesare's jealousy of Juan, and the supposed incestuous relationships within the family. Incest is a theme that shows itself time and again in the story of Cesare and Lucrezia, none of which has any basis in fact. In the very same way, there is absolutely no concrete contemporary evidence that Cesare had a hand in his brother's murder. The two may have had a relationship that was full of envy and dislike, but it cannot be discounted that the family was close and that fratricide would have marred the relationship between Cesare and his father. Sibling rivalry, therefore, is hardly a substantial reason for murder. Rather it seems far more likely that one of Juan's many enemies, most likely the Orsinis, were the ones who committed the foul deed and ended Gandia's life.

We can therefore be reasonably certain that Cesare Borgia had no hand in his brother's death. At any rate, Cesare was quickly riding off to Naples in order to crown King Federigo and he arrived by 2 August 1497, briefly falling ill shortly after. He was sufficiently recovered enough to crown the king on 11 August, in a magnificent ceremony. But despite the ostentation of the service, the barons of Naples who opposed the Aragonese dynasty completely boycotted the whole thing. Cesare had not only been sent to crown the king but also to try and create peace between these nobles and the House of Aragon. It was all somewhat of a failure. But despite not being able to broker peace, Cesare had another job to do whilst in Naples and that was to look into securing an Aragonese match for the soon to be divorced Lucrezia.

Cesare came away from Naples with much more than he bargained for, however. Far from being the perfect Churchman whilst in the City, he had of course sampled its delights. Amidst his extravagant spending, King Federigo was forced to bear the brunt of Cesare's flamboyant court. This was, after all, the same young man whose extravagance had been noted whilst he was still a student in Pisa. His spending and enjoyment led, of course, to him tasting the delights of the women of Naples – the very same women who had proven to be so alluring to Charles VIII and his army not so many years previously.

Upon his return to Rome from Naples, Cesare found himself to be the victim of the notorious 'French Disease'. Syphilis was first noted following the French occupation of Naples and, as such, the people of Italy named it 'The French Disease' – the French, however, called it the 'Italian Disease'. Naples was, therefore, the epicentre of the outbreak. But how was it spread by the invading French? It is thought that the disease was originally transmitted through Spanish mercenaries serving under Charles VIII, who caught it in the New World and then spread it amongst the citizens of Naples who then ended up infecting the invading French soldiers. The French then spread it further and thus it began to creep across Europe. The disease at the time was incredibly lethal and led to thousands and thousands of people developing it and its deformities, even leading to widespread death.[16] Indeed, many well-known individuals around this time suffered with the illness, including Cardinal della Roverre and Francesco Gonzaga. This disease was something that would affect Cesare Borgia for much of the remainder of his life, both physically and in the form of rumour that would even haunt his memory long after his death

Chapter 6

Throwing off the Crimson

I n the aftermath of Juan's death, Lucrezia's reputation was once more dragged through the mud. There were whispers that she had been involved, sexually, with one of Alexander's Spanish chamberlains, Pedro Calderon – known more familiarly as Perotto. The young chamberlain suddenly disappeared and Johannes Burchard, the Papal Master of Ceremonies notes in his diary that the young man 'fell not of his own will into the Tiber'.[1] Rumours circulated the city that he had been murdered for getting Lucrezia pregnant and that he was the reason she had been closeted away in San Sisto – so she could give birth to the child she was apparently carrying. His rotting corpse was allegedly found alongside the body of one of Lucrezia's serving women, Pantisilea – could it be that she knew of the supposed affair and was murdered to make sure there was no evidence left anywhere?

The murder of Perotto was later attributed to Cesare in an overly sensational manner and the tale has since become an unshakeable part of the Borgia myth. The story goes that Cesare, fuelled with rage that a lowly chamberlain should have taken his sister in such a way, pursued Perotto through the halls of the Vatican. Perotto threw himself at what he thought was the safety of the Pontiff's robes. As he clung to Alexander's papal vestments, Cesare plunged the dagger over and over into the back of the chamberlain with such force that his blood spattered all across the fabric of Alexander's clothing.[2] Ferrara states that this event is only mentioned in an anonymous letter sent to the exiled Silvio Savelli, a letter that was written to not only blacken the Borgia name, but destroy their reputation entirely. This letter is a source that truly cannot be trusted – it is a compendium of stories from those who despised the Borgia family and wanted their reputation completely soiled.

The whole Perotto affair was only made worse, and Lucrezia's reputation soiled even further, with the appearance of a new baby within the walls of the Vatican. This child, Giovanni Borgia, became known as the *Infans Romanus* and rumours circulated that the child was Lucrezia's and had been born during her seclusion in San Sisto. Officially, the child's paternity was attributed to Cesare; however, in a secret bull dated to September 1502, Alexander admitted that the child was actually his.

But despite this scandal, a new marriage for Lucrezia was of the utmost importance. Alexander once more began to negotiate with Naples – he had, after all, already had Gioffre married into the Neapolitan royal family – and wished for Lucrezia to marry King Federigo's illegitimate son, Alfonso. But Federigo began to prove difficult, not particularly wanting to have more of his children marry into the Pope's family. Alexander was understandably furious at the whole situation and in retaliation, told the king that Lucrezia would actually marry Francesco Orsini. He kept up the pretence whilst negotiations continued, until Alfonso arrived secretly in Rome and an agreement was finally reached – Alfonso and Lucrezia were to marry. Alfonso was given the Duchy of Bisceglie whilst Lucrezia brought with her a dowry of 40,000 ducats.[3]

Just a few days later, on 21 July, the two were married and Lucrezia became Duchess of Bisceglie. It soon became very clear that the newly married couple were head over heels in love with each other. During the celebrations, a fight broke out between two bishops and swords were drawn – once it had all died down the family sat down for a magnificent wedding breakfast. Part way through the feast, Cesare appeared dressed as a unicorn and danced during a performance. Other members of the family also joined in with this magnificent celebration – Gioffre was dressed as a sea goose and Cardinal Juan Borgia Lanzol as an elephant.[4] Sancia's account describes the celebrations in all their glory, describing how those dressed as animals even wore costumes that matched the colour of their chosen creatures. She describes how they danced one by one in front of the Pope, before drinking from a special fountain and then, once they had all had a drink they danced as a group.[5] Cesare presided over the majority of the celebrations – not only were there days and days of dancing and feasting, but he also organised a huge bullfight. Ten thousand spectators attended the event and Cesare himself appeared on the field. Sancia, Cesare's sister in law and mistress, reported that he was accompanied by a beautifully dressed Barbary horse and that throughout the afternoon Cesare killed every single bull that he faced.[6]

Despite the celebrations, politics hadn't taken a backseat and Alexander's thoughts were turning towards securing a marriage for Cesare. Originally, Alexander had wanted to secure the Neapolitan king's natural daughter, Carlotta, for Cesare but Federigo was proving difficult. It didn't help that Federigo was traditionally allied with the Spanish king and queen, Ferdinand and Isabella – the monarchs were strongly opposed to Cesare leaving the College of Cardinals and had refused to give the lands that had once belonged to Juan, to Cesare. It was even reported that Cesare would not leave the Cardinalate, due to not getting the answers he wanted. Yet just three weeks later, it was reported that Cesare would indeed go through with his plan, despite what the Spanish monarchs said.[7] Cesare was evidently hesitant to throw off his Cardinal's robes and step into the role of soldier. Whilst at this point he was often seen practicing his swordsmanship, he still attended church though it was so rare that Burchard commented on it in his diaries, stating that Cesare hadn't been seen in church since Passion Sunday.[8] It would be the last time that Cesare was seen in church, though he seemed to still be on the fence about whether or not to leave the College of Cardinals. Yet Alexander pushed him and began to work even harder at finding a wife for his son – he began to probe an alliance with France and negotiations began. Unfortunately, the untimely death of Charles VIII on 7 April 1498 put an end to those negotiations.

Charles died after entering a darkened hallway in order to visit a group of artists whom he had employed to decorate a part of the palace of Amboise. As he ducked through the doorway, he struck his head so hard that he fell into a stupor. He died that very same day, aged just twenty-eight years old. Phillipe de Commines describes the king's death in his memoirs and how at times Charles recovered his speech:

'The Bishop of Angers, and the gentleman of his bed-chamber, who were then about him, told me what I write: The last expression he used whilst he was in health was, that he hoped never to commit a mortal sin again, nor a venial sin if he could help it; and with this words in his mouth he fell down backwards and lost his speech. It was about two in the afternoon when he fell, and he lay motionless till eleven o'clock at night. Thrice he recovered his speech, but he quickly lost it again...The confessor told me that every time he recovered his speech he called out upon God, the glorious Virgin Mary, St. Claude, and St. Blaise, to assist him. And thus died that great and powerful monarch in a sordid and filthy place'[9]

Charles's successor was Louis, Duke d'Orleans and it was a huge stroke of good luck for Alexander in Rome. Louis desperately needed the Pope's help – he wanted to divorce his wife Jeanne de France and to marry Charles's widow, Anne of Brittany. He couldn't do either of these things without a special dispensation from the Pope. Not only that but Louis had a claim to both Naples and Milan – if he were to take hold of these places, then he needed Alexander's blessing. It was the perfect opportunity for the Borgias to get what they wanted.

In the June of 1498, Louis had an envoy sent to the Papal court in order to ask for a dissolution of his marriage. Alexander, at the same time, sent his own envoy to the Court of France and on 29 July, Alexander agreed for a tribunal to examine the case for the dissolution of the king's marriage. An agreement was also reached in which Louis would support Cesare's wish for a Neapolitan marriage to Carlotta. Cesare would also be given the Duchies of Valence and Dios, the command of 100 of the King's soldiers, a yearly stipend of 20,000 gold francs and he would be invested with the Order of St Michael.[10]

Everything was falling into place. Cesare was about to embark on the next stage of his career – a career which would have absolutely nothing to do with being a Cardinal. When news arrived in Rome that Louis was sending the patents for Cesare's investiture as Duke of Valentinois and Diois, the final decision was made. On Friday 17 August 1498, he publicly announced that he would be leaving the College of Cardinals. He made his announcement to a half empty room – many had refused to come and left the city, fearing that their consciences would get the better of them. Burchard reports in his diary that Cesare told the gathered Cardinals that he only agreed to enter the Church as he believed it was his father's will but that he was more inclined to the secular life.[11] Alexander was furious that so many Cardinals had refused to come, so he organised for another consistory to be held. And this time he wrote to the absent Cardinals and demanded that they attend. With no choice but to obey, they attended and voted that Cesare could indeed leave the College of Cardinals – Cesare Borgia was now free to pursue a military career and take a wife. The future of the Borgia dynasty now rested solely on his shoulders.

The die was cast. That same day, the patents that gave Cesare the Duchy of Valence arrived. The Cardinal of Valencia could now call himself the Duc de' Valentinois and so, the infamous 'Valentino' was born. Gone were the crimson robes of the Cardinal – now he had the secular life that he dreamed of, and the friendship of the king of France. Everything was falling into place and at just twenty-three years of age, Cesare Borgia was about to begin a stage of his life that would turn into a legend.

To celebrate his movement away from the Church, Cesare had a beautiful sword made for himself. The design on the blade was full of allusions to Cesare's links to Julius Caesar as well as his own power – all across the blade are Borgia emblems, as well as the name Cesar. There are also beautiful scenes including one which shows Caesar crossing the Rubicon with his famous '*iacta alea est*' (The Die is Cast) saying inscribed beneath. Other scenes depict the famous triumph of Caesar and the ideas of Faith, Peace and Love. A beautiful leather scabbard was also made for the sword and is currently held in the Victoria and Albert Museum in London. Whilst it was never used, the scabbard is also decorated with scenes and monograms showing Cesare's links to

Caesar, his personal emblems and the goddess of peace. On one side are scenes showing the worship and a sacrifice of a ram to the deity, above which is the imperial eagle. The designs on this side, however, are incomplete. On the reverse are a number of Caesar monograms and groups of three flames which were the personal emblem of Cesare. The scabbard is also inscribed with the saying '*Materium superabit Opus*' This is usually translated as 'The workmanship was better than the subject matter', a phrase which was penned by the Roman poet, Ovid. Cesare had a particular interest in classical history and wanted to show himself as just as great, if not more so, than Julius Caesar. The sword and scabbard were made for ceremonial purposes rather than to be used in warfare, and it was a symbol of nobility to be able to wear such an imposing piece during peacetime – the use of personal emblems would have also reinforced his status as a man of power. The scabbard remained unfinished, however, and on the reverse side there are splits in the leather.[12] Each and every scene on both the sword and the scabbard has a personal meaning for Cesare and represented his own crossing of the Rubicon in his move from the Church to the secular life. He practically hero worshipped Julius Caesar and wanted to match Caesar's military triumphs, even going so far as to have a motto inscribed on his scabbard invoking his namesake's protection.[13]

Cesare now began to make preparations for the next big step in his life and started to train physically – harder than he ever had before – in order to impress the French court when he finally made it there. His preparations including bullfighting on horseback – one instance of this happened the day after he had formally left the College of Cardinals. The Mantuan ambassador Cattaneo reported on this event:

'Armed as a janissary, with another fourteen men, he gave many proofs of strength in killing eight bulls…in a few days, I hope to see him fully armed on the piazza'[14]

There were times, however, when Cesare took his physical exercise too far and got himself hurt. Cattaneo reported on 29 August that on the previous evening, Cesare had tried in one leap to:

'Mount a mule rather taller than the rest…and when he was in the air the mule took fright and kicked him in the ribs and on the back of the head, and he lay unconscious for more than an hour.'[15]

But despite the work Cesare was putting in to make sure he was physically fit and able to wow the French court, he was starting to grow increasingly more worried about his appearance. Cesare's face was beginning to once again show signs of the ravaging illness of syphilis – Cattaneo reported that:

'He is well enough in countenance at present, although he has his face blotched beneath the skin as is usual with the Great Pox'[16]

At just twenty three years of age, and as a young man obsessed with his own appearance, it must have been an incredibly difficult situation for Cesare. It is likely that he had originally thought himself cured of the dreaded disease after its disappearance previously and, as syphilis was a new phenomenon introduced by the invading French army, he could not have known that the unsightly rash brought on by the secondary stage would have disappeared within a few months. Still, in a letter at this time he signed himself as 'Cardinal Valentinus' – his insecurities were starting to show themselves and it is possible that he believed the changes in his looks would put a spanner in his plans for marring a noblewoman at the French Court. Even Cattaneo reported on Cesare's inability to fully embrace his future in the secular world:

'Valencia has certainly left in lay clothes, and having made his preparations as Duke, nonetheless he signed himself up to the last moment as Cesar, Card. Valentino…and this perhaps as a precaution if things did not come out as he wished or that perhaps, because of that face of his, spoiled by the French disease, his wife might refuse him.'[17]

There were other factors that may have had some influence on Cesare's reluctance to fully give up signing himself as Cardinal. He was, after all, playing an incredibly dangerous game. Now that the Borgia family had turned their back on Naples and the Spanish alliance, the Spanish king was exceptionally displeased that the family had turned to France. Many even warned Pope Alexander that Louis XII would simply treat Cesare as a hostage, rather than an ally. They warned, as Cattaneo reported, that Louis wanted Cesare because he did not trust the Pope.[18] Alexander was taking a massive gamble, but it was in his nature to do such a thing – the risks certainly did not outweigh the gaining of Cesare's power, so he continued with the game, utterly determined to wow the French king with the splendour and ostentation of the Papal Court.

A huge amount of money was spent on the preparations for Cesare's departure – 200,000 ducats had been raised, the money having partly been confiscated from a bishop who had recently been condemned for heresy. Cesare's suite was to be made up of over 100 individuals and the horses of his followers were magnificently outfitted with bridles of solid silver, whilst the followers themselves were dressed in the most magnificent livery. Cesare was also accompanied by Ramiro de Lorqua, the Spanish master of his household, his secretary Agapito Geraldini and his physician Gaspare Torella, the only man who had studied, and come up with a treatment for, syphilis at that point. He was also to be accompanied by an escort of honour made up of thirty noble gentlemen including Giangiordano Orsini and Gianbattista Mancini. Cesare departed on 1 October 1498, followed by his magnificent train. He was dressed to the nines in a white doublet of damask laced with gold and a black velvet mantle over his shoulders. He also wore a cap of black velvet emblazoned with rubies.[19] His twelve baggage carts and fifty baggage mules were full to bursting with riches and, according to Cattaneo, Cesare also took with him a travelling privy 'covered with gold brocade without and scarlet within, with silver vessels within the silver urinals'.[20]

Cesare's ostentatious display was described as 'without pomp' by Burchard, yet his whole display utterly disgusted the French Court when he arrived. Indeed, he would completely change his way of dressing during his time in France – when he returned to Italy, he would dress only in black velvet.

Cesare and his entourage landed at Marseilles on 12 October 1498, where they were met by the Bishop of Dijon and a group of 400 military archers as a mark of honour. Following a few days spent in Marseilles where he was shown the sights of the town as well as the relics of St Lazaire (whose name, ironically, was linked to syphilis in Italy), Cesare was accompanied to Avignon by the Bishop of Dijon where he was greeted by Cardinal Giuliano della Roverre. Despite della Roverre's dislike for the Borgia Pope, he and Cesare seemed to be on amicable terms for the moment, particularly as della Roverre was to play a part in the upcoming negotiations which would result in his return to influence in Rome. Della Roverre even made a show of this amicability by riding two miles out of Avignon to meet his guest and led him back into the city where Borgia was greeted with a raucous display including fountains spouting wine, dancing and magnificent parties.

Cesare tarried at Avignon likely due to a recurrence of the Great Pox. Della Roverre, who also suffered with the malady, had also fallen sick. But once recovered, the cardinal accompanied Cesare and his entourage on their journey to Chinon, where Cesare was to be met by the French king. On the way, he stopped at the capital of his new Duchy in Valence. He did not make a good impression there, proving himself to be an aloof and overly pretentious young man – when, during a reception, a representative of Louis XII came forward with the collar of the Order of St Michael and made to place it about Cesare's neck, he pushed it away and stated that he would only accept it from the king's hands.

When on 17 December it was announced that the divorce commission had found in Louis' favour, preparations were made for Cesare to finally enter Chinon. Louis was free of his marriage and the divorced wife entered a convent. The following day, Cesare entered Chinon mounted on a magnificent warhorse and was dressed in black, with the slashed sleeves on his doublet showing gold beneath. About his neck hung a pendant of diamonds said to be worth 30,000 ducats and on his head

was the same ruby emblazoned black velvet cap. Even his boots, made
of black velvet, were emblazoned with gold thread and gems.[21]

He was greeted on the bridge leading into Chinon by the Bishop of
Rouen, George d'Amboise, as well as several other gentlemen of the
court. They escorted him through the town to the castle of Chinon
where Cesare was greeted warmly by Louis XII. The medieval fortress,
a temporary stop for the French Court, was the very same castle in
which Joan of Arc had met Charles VII and urged him to save France.
The French Court was always on the move and would go on to Blois
following their stay at Chinon.

But Cesare was not there simply to win the approval of the king of
France – he was there to find a wife, and he wanted to win Carlotta of
Naples' hand in marriage. When Cesare first came face to face with
Carlotta, who was serving as one of the queen's ladies, she stated that she
had absolutely no intention of becoming known as 'La Cardinala' and,
unfortunately for Cesare, Carlotta was having none of it and showed no
interest in his overtures – she was in love with another, a young Breton
gentleman who was in the service of Anne of Brittany. Quite simply,
Cesare didn't stand a chance. Cesare was not one to give up easily,
however. He made sure to win over the rest of the court in the meantime
and he became particularly close to Louis and, as he began to feel at
home, he began to feel more and more self-confident, showing himself
as having the natural ability to get on well with practically everyone in
the court. Louis himself believed that Cesare was a considerable asset to
both his court and his friendship. But that wasn't enough for Cesare –
the only result that mattered to him was securing a wife and the future
of the Borgia dynasty.

On 6 January 1499, Louis XII married Anne of Brittany in the castle
of Nantes and, to show just how grateful he was to Cesare for helping to
bring about the marriage, bestowed upon him the Lordship of Issouden.
But despite Louis' happiness over his marriage, Cesare's marital future
looked to be an impossibility – Carlotta was still stubbornly refusing to
even consider a marriage to Cesare Borgia, despite Louis stepping in

and trying to convince her. The news, reported to Alexander in a letter by Giuliano della Roverre on 18 January, greatly perturbed the Pope who stated in a reply that if the marriage did not happen, then he would be the laughing stock of all Italy. Cesare must have been perturbed also and showed signs of wishing to return to Rome but he could not without a wife. So he stayed and hoped that Louis could come through for him and secure the marriage that he so desperately wished for.

Louis tried hard to press the matter when Neapolitan envoys arrived, yet even they refused to sanction the idea of Cesare marrying Carlotta, stating that 'to a bastard son of the Pope, the King would not give his legitimate daughter, but not even a bastard child'.[22]

Louis dismissed them on the spot and demanded that Carlotta attend a meal with him, the queen and Cesare in which he made one last ditch attempt to convince Carlotta to marry the duke. But nothing could be done and Giuliano della Roverre reported to the Pope that there was no chance at all of a wedding between the two going ahead.

It seemed as if all of Cesare's hopes were turning to bitter disappointments. But he was not out of the game just yet and he was determined to leave France with not only a marriage, but an alliance that would help him take control of Italy.

Chapter 7

The Bull and the Tigress

A new bride had to be found for Cesare after Carlotta's continued refusal to even think about marrying him. There can be no doubt at all that her refusal to marry him would have stung his pride to its very core – Cesare was already a proud young man who could not deal with any sort of insult, so this must have been double the hurt for him. Still, Cesare threw himself into the politics of the French court with absolute gusto, working himself hard with Louis to find a new bride. And when Louis presented his cousin, Charlotte d'Albret, Cesare was seemingly delighted.

Charlotte D'Albret was born in around 1483 at the d'Albret family castle of Nerac to Francois de Bretagne, a kinswoman of the queen, and Alain d'Albret who was Duke of Guyenne and held a slew of other titles. Moreover, Charlotte's older brother Jean had inherited the crown of Navarre. We know little of Charlotte's childhood but we do know that she came from an incredibly rich family – the lady of Nerac and her daughters were provided with beautiful fabrics for gowns including velvet and damask, jewels and sumptuous nightwear.[1] Whilst little is known of her childhood, we do know that by the age of sixteen, Charlotte was an acknowledged beauty.

However much Cesare was delighted with the prospect of marrying Charlotte, her father was less enthusiastic about the match and made sure to drag out the negotiations and squeeze as much out of both Louis and the Borgia Pope as was humanly possible. Nothing is recorded about Charlotte's feelings on the marriage, however the negotiations for her dowry were conducted as little more than a livestock sale – perhaps he was trying to put the Borgia family off the idea of the marriage. As one French historian put it, it would be 'a veritable crime, to have abandoned to the most corrupt of Italian princes a young girl of such beauty, such piety, and such sweetness'.[2] Alain d'Albret demanded 100,000 livres for the dowry to be paid in ducats, to see the dispensation that allowed Cesare to marry as well as a number of other guarantees. Whilst the Borgias and Louis agreed to most of Alain's demands, they also provided a Cardinal's hat for Charlotte's brother and a place in the Parliament of Bordeaux for Alain's chief representative. With everything agreed, the marriage contract was signed on 10 May 1499, at Blois.

The wedding took place two days later, in the queen's closet at Blois in a quiet and simple ceremony. It was, however, followed up with a magnificent wedding breakfast hosted by the groom himself in the gardens of the chateau. And that afternoon, whilst the party was still in full swing, the marriage of Cesare Borgia and Charlotte d'Albret was consummated. The whole affair proved to be an amusing one for Charlotte's ladies who spied on the two through the keyhole of their bedroom door, but the whole thing was spoiled with a rather amusing incident described by Robert de la Marck:

'To tell you of the Duke of Valence's wedding night, he asked the apothecary for some pills to pleasure his lady. But he received a bad turn for, instead of giving him what he asked for, the apothecary gave him laxative pills which had such an effect that he never ceased going to the privy for the whole night.'[3]

The very next day Cesare sent a letter to his father boasting that he had broken the lance eight times, a feat so exceptional that Burchard even mentions it in his diary.[4] Cesare reported that following the wedding he was 'the most contented man in the world' whilst Charlotte wrote to both her father and the Pope to say that she was extremely satisfied with her new husband.[5] Her satisfaction may be down to the fact that her husband was considered to be one of the most handsome men in all of Italy, but it may also have been due to her receiving a number of sumptuous gifts from Cesare. These gifts – made up of brocade, silk and jewels – had been meant for Carlotta d'Aragona. Whether Charlotte knew of this is not known, however her satisfaction over the gifts and her marriage was certainly evident.

Just a week after the wedding, Cesare was invested formally with the order of St Michael and Louis continued to lavish gifts and titles upon him. His worry over potentially going back into the Church was over and from that moment on, Cesare proudly signed himself as 'Cesare Borgia of France, Duke of Valentinois'. Everything had fallen into place for Cesare Borgia – now all he needed to do was gain an army and begin building an empire for his father, the Pope.

In Rome, Cesare's marriage was marked with celebrations. Lucrezia herself, pregnant with her first child with Alfonso d'Aragona, lit a huge bonfire in celebration. But not everyone was happy with the newly cemented alliance. As news trickled through to Rome that Cesare was to command a unit of French cavalry on Louis' trip to Italy, Ascanio Sforza fled Rome under the pretext of going on a hunting trip. When Ludovico Sforza captured one of Cesare's messengers, Ascanio quickly left his hiding place at Nettuno to join his brother in Milan. Lucrezia's husband, Alfonso d'Aragona, secretly left Rome on 2 August and joined the Colonna at Genezzano, leaving behind his tearful wife who was six months pregnant. Even Sancia left for Naples, leaving behind her young husband Gioffre Borgia who was locked in the Castel Sant Angelo after taking part in a skirmish which left a member of the city police severely wounded.

Alfonso wrote to his pregnant wife, begging her to join him. However, the letter fell into the Pope's hands, thanks to an excellent intelligence system housed within the walls of the Vatican. The Pope, in order to stop his daughter from joining her husband, sent her off to the small town of Spoleto, where she was to act as its governor. It was an appointment that showed just how much Pope Alexander trusted his daughter – it was her first foray into politics, and she would prove herself to be an excellent governor. Alexander even wrote to the priors of Spoleto, making it clear just how much he trusted Lucrezia in her new role:

'Dear Sons: Greeting and the Apostolic Blessing! We have entrusted to our beloved daughter in Christ, the noble lady, Lucretia de Borgia Duchess of Biseglia, the office of keeper of the castle, as well as the government of our cities of Spoleto and Foligno, and of the country and district about them. Having perfect confidence in the intelligence, the fidelity, and probity of the Duchess, which We have swelt upon in previous letters, and likewise in your unfailing obedience to Us and to the Holy See, We trust that you will receive the Duchess Lucretia, as is your duty, with all due honour as your regent, and show her submission in all things. As we wish her to be received and accepted by you with special honour and respect, so do We command you in this epistle – as you value Our favour and wish to avoid Our displeasure – to obey the Duchess Lucretia, your regent, in all things collectively and severally, in so far as law and custom dictate in government of the city, and whatever she may think proper to exact of you, even as you would obey Ourselves, and to execute her commands with all diligence and promptness, so that your devotion may receive due approbation. Given in Rome, in St. Peter's, under the papal seal, August 8, 1499.'[6]

Gioffre accompanied his sister to Spoleto along with by a group of pages who were under strict instructions not to let him out of their sight. Although he had been released from his imprisonment in the Castel Sant Angelo, Gioffre Borgia was little more than a prisoner.

Lucrezia and Gioffre set out on 8 August followed by forty-three coaches, a number of noblemen and ladies in waiting, soldiers and attendants. Lucrezia travelled in a litter outfitted with mattresses and cushions, provided for her by the Pope on account of her condition – as they set out from the Santa Maria in Portico, Pope Alexander came out to salute the new Governor of Spoleto and wave goodbye to his children. The party entered Spoleto on 14 August to a large crowd who cheered the arrival of their new governor and made their way towards the fortress where Lucrezia was greeted by her new court. Once settled in, Lucrezia handed the briefs from the Pontifical Chancellery over to the Priors of Spoleto and gave audiences to the magistrates in her magnificent hall of honour. She proved herself to be a patient mistress in listening to the complaints and petitions of her people.[7] And things had begun to look up for her prospects in seeing her husband again, too. On 20 August, the Spanish Commander Juan Cervillon, a man who had been a witness at Lucrezia's wedding, went to Naples with a message from Alexander, to negotiate the return of Alfonso to Rome. It was eventually decided that Alfonso d'Aragona, Duke of Bisceglie, should re-join his wife in September – the relationship between Lucrezia and Alfonso was about to enter its final act.

Meanwhile, Cesare had taken leave of his wife to join Louis and his army at Lyon. Charlotte d'Albret would never see her husband again. From Lyon, the army set out to conquer Italy and on 6 October 1499, Louis XII entered Milan as a conqueror. The victory had been easy – Ludovico Sforza had fled the city as the French had borne down upon his duchy. And as the French advanced, the great Italian lords had rushed to join them just as they had with Louis' predecessor. It was better, after all, to be on the side of the army that was winning. Louis' entry into Milan was a splendid one, fitting for the king he was. But the people of Milan did not receive Louis and his army warmly at all. Instead, they were quiet for the most part – the loudest shouts were towards the representatives of Venice, who the people of Milan despised. When Louis entered the Castello Sforzesco, he found that the chests that had been designed by Leonardo da Vinci to hold Ludovico's gold had been entirely emptied – Ludovico took with him 240,000 gold ducats and the majority of his collection of jewels.[8] He had however, left enough for the French to be suitably impressed and the day after arriving in the city, Louis went to visit Da Vinci's famous fresco of the Last Supper in the monastery of Santa Maria della Grazie. The fresco, painted between 1494 and 1498, was completed in a very different way to traditional frescoes – Da Vinci painted it on dry, rather than on wet plaster, and because of this, by the time Louis visited the fresco, the paint was already beginning to deteriorate.

Cesare had fulfilled his part of the bargain and helped Louis to take Milan. Now it was time for Louis to fulfil his own part of the bargain and provide Cesare with an army. Father and son came up with a thinly veiled excuse, stating that they needed the troops to reassert dominance in the Papal States. These states all belonged to the Church and many were ruled by lords who were known as vicars. The Papal States, which covered a large section of North and Central Italy, were areas rife with crime, with the ruling lords resorting to cruelty in order to maintain order. Pope Alexander wanted the area brought under control so that it could be made into one huge duchy for his son and he began this mission by announcing that:

'The vicars of Rimini, Pesaro, Imola, Forli, Camerino and Faenza, as well as the Duke of Urbino, feudatories of the Church in Rome, have failed to pay their annual census to the Apostolic Chamber.'[9]

As punishment, Alexander removed the titles of these vicars and declared them forfeit. Louis, in Milan, also lent 45,000 ducats to the Pope in order to raise troops to retake these territories. Lucrezia had returned to Rome in the October and, on 1 November, gave birth to a baby boy who was christened Rodrigo.

Cesare was about to fully cross his own personal Rubicon. Whilst the first step had already been made in his marriage to Charlotte d'Albret, the eyes of both the Pope and Cesare were now on the Romagna – it was their aim to turn it into Cesare's very own kingdom and at that moment, nothing else mattered. For now, even the issue of Lucrezia's marriage to Alfonso d'Aragona was pushed to the back of their minds. Cesare's eye had fallen on Imola and Forli, held and ruled by the ruthless virago, Caterina Sforza Riario, and he set out with his army to begin the taking of her lands.

Born in Milan in 1463, Caterina Sforza was the illegitimate daughter of Duke Galeazzo Maria Sforza and his mistress Lucrezia Landriani. As with the Borgia children, Caterina's illegitimacy did not prove to be an issue in her future prospects. Indeed she was brought up in her father's household alongside his legitimate children and given an education perfect for the daughter of a duke and was surrounded by art and music. Not only that, she descended from a family of celebrated condottieri and grew up watching her family fight and take lands by force – Galeazzo Sforza took Imola in 1471, a territory which Caterina herself would come to rule over in the future. In January 1473, Caterina was married to Girolamo Riario, the Duke of Imola in a quiet ceremony – she was just eleven years old at the time of her marriage and the consummation that took place following the ceremony was considered to be illegal (generally, both parties had to be over the age of fourteen or so to be considered of age and suitable for consummation). Riario's uncle, Pope Sixtus IV, hastily signed a papal bull on February 26 1476, which declared the marriage to be completely valid and cleared all parties of any wrong doing in the illegal consummation of the marriage.[10] Caterina was no stranger to heartbreak, however. Her father was assassinated in Milan's magnificent cathedral on 26 December 1476 and, many years later, Caterina watched as her husband was brutally murdered by the Orsi clan and fanatic members of the people of Forli.

Caterina Sforza was no stranger to taking control, either. At the age of just twenty-four, she had held the Castel Sant' Angelo during the violent interregnum that followed Pope Sixtus' death. And following the brutal murder of her husband in 1488, she held the Rocca de Ravaldino in Forli against the people of the town. When the rebels brought one of her children to the outside of the castle, it is said that she lifted her skirts and declared that they could kill her son as she had the means to make many more.[11] Such moments in her life only prepared her to take control – and it was the control, particularly of Forli and the protection of her son Ottaviano's inheritance, that would turn her into the very tigress who would show her claws to Cesare Borgia.

But before he could even reach Imola, Caterina's other town, Cesare was forced to turn and rush straight back to Rome. Caterina, ever the wily one, had completely pre-empted Cesare's attack by attempting to poison the Pope. On that very afternoon, one of Gioffre Borgia's musicians was carted off to the Castel Sant'Angelo, accused with trying to murder the Pope by means of letters wrapped in a shroud that had covered the body of a plague victim. Another version of the story has the letters being soaked in poison. The plot had failed and Cesare, who had arrived secretly at the Vatican, spent three days locked away with his father discussing his next move on Caterina and her towns.

The people of Imola and Forli did not fight Cesare – as with the other towns that he had taken, they simply just handed over control. The Venetian diarist Sanuto states that they gave themselves to Il Valentino 'like whores'.[12] Cesare entered the city of Imola on 27 November and a week later, after heavy bombardments, the citadel surrendered. It had been the last, and really the only, part of the city that had not immediately surrendered. On 15 December, Cesare left Imola and headed for Forli where he would come face to face with the virago who held the imposing Rocca de Ravaldino. He entered Forli on 17 December in a torrential rainstorm, with a lance held at rest in the style of the conquering hero that he so wished to be. Caterina Sforza, meanwhile, held Ravaldino. Following his entry into the town, the soldiers that had followed Cesare began to pillage – the French and Gascon soldiers raped and pillaged their way through Forli and, as the men only answered to their French commanders, he was utterly powerless to stop them. Cesare, on the other hand, was more than courteous to the people of the town, allowing them to remain in their homes. He certainly was not a monster in that sense of the word, but rather showed himself as a patient and exceptional ruler.

Caterina held out in Ravaldino and, the day after Christmas, Cesare made two personal attempts to get her to surrender. Both failed. He rode to the moat surrounding the fortress and tried to get her to come out on the ramparts to talk to him. Sforza lowered the drawbridge and made to trap Cesare by lifting it when he rode onto it – he jumped free at the last moment. Then, utterly furious, he shouted myriad obscenities and told his camp that he would reward 1,000 ducats to anyone who captured Caterina dead or alive. Her stubbornness meant that he knew he had to fight to get her out – and fight he did. On 10 January, he began bombarding the walls of the fortress once more – two days later, the walls of the imposing building had been breached. Cesare now ordered the assault and the first through the breach were the French and Gascon troops. Surprisingly, they were not met with resistance. Indeed, many of Caterina's soldiers had begun to desert her. Only Caterina and her remaining loyal men were left and she certainly managed to live up to her reputation in the fight that ensued. She herself strode out to meet the invaders followed by a few who remained loyal to her, fighting bravely in the front ranks with her sword in hand, showing herself truly to be the daughter of the feared Sforza condottiere. After fighting hard for more than two hours, she ordered her men to collect up everything flammable that they could get their hands on and create a wall of fire. It didn't keep the invaders back for long – they broke the wall down and advanced through the smoke, whilst many of Caterina's remaining men surrendered. Caterina would do no such thing. She sealed the entry gate and ordered those left to prepare for a siege.

When the news reached Cesare's ears that Caterina had once again locked herself away, he had one last hand to play. He rode up to the keep and a herald summoned her out onto the ramparts to speak with him. As he spoke, he begged her to see sense. But as she made to retort and demand that he show respect to her people, a hand fell on her shoulder and words were whispered in her ear stating that she was now a prisoner of the Constable of Dijon. When it came down to it, Caterina had not been taken by Cesare Borgia. She had been betrayed from within the walls of her very own castle.

Cesare did not immediately enter Ravaldino upon the capture of Caterina Sforza Riario. Instead he waited for the building to be completely subdued. Once inside, however, Cesare did not find it easy to get his hands on the woman who had held the fortress against him.

The French soldier who had captured Caterina demanded that he be paid the reward Cesare had promised – Borgia immediately handed over 2,000 ducats but was promptly reminded that he had upped the reward amount to the huge sum of 10,000 ducats. When Cesare lost his temper, the Frenchman held a dagger to Caterina's throat and threatened to present Cesare with just her head, if he did not receive the full amount of money. Then the French Commander Yves D'Allegre stepped in, jumping to the defence of his soldier and declaring that Caterina Sforza Riario was now under the protection of King Louis XII of France. That way, she could not be tortured, imprisoned or killed – which was probably the fate that awaited her if she were to fall into Borgia hands. But this was not good enough for Cesare. He had fought too hard to lose out on his prize now and insisted that she be handed over to him for safekeeping – technically she would still be under the protection of the French king and would just be being looked after by Cesare. But Cesare was too wily a soldier and statesman to stick to the promise that he had made. She was handed over to him at just gone midnight and, as she was led through the carnage she commented that the fate of those left living upset her far more than the fate of the dead. Those that survived had been handed over to the soldiers who had won the day, the women likely to be used for their bodies whilst many other prisoners had simply just been killed. At least the dead, she commented, had died with honour. She was then taken to the house of Luffo Numai, the very man who had welcomed Cesare into Forli, where Cesare waited for his prize to be brought to him. He sat eating a hearty meal and drinking wine as Caterina was brought to him – he had hoped that her children would be brought to him also but she told him, perhaps with some element of smugness, that she had removed the heirs to Imola and Forli to safety in Florence before the siege had even begun.

Rumour abounded that Cesare abused his Sforza captive, raping her and violating her body and it was said that the morning after Cesare boasted that she had 'defended her fortresses better than her virtue'.[13] Other sources, however, make no mention of the supposed rape whatsoever. However such a thing cannot be ruled out. Cesare, after all, had a cruel streak and would have thought little about taking her honour and virtue, after she had proven that she did not respect, or even fear him.

Nine days after Cesare had finally taken Ravaldino, he moved on to begin the siege of Pesaro. Pesaro was the home and dominion of Giovanni Sforza, Cesare's one time brother-in-law who had been utterly humiliated by the Borgia family. Cesare, of course, took his new prize with him. But as they were travelling along the Via Emilia, they found the way blocked by Yves d'Allegre and his contingent of French infantry. Allegre had been slighted by Cesare when he had taken Caterina and was concerned that Borgia would simply just kill her whilst on their journey. When Allegre claimed custody of Caterina, Cesare simply handed her over before rushing off towards Cesena, whilst she was sent back to Forli. But freedom was not on the cards for Caterina Sforza Riario and Cesare Borgia would not take the loss of his momentous prize lying down. The very next day he made his way back to Forli to discuss the options for Caterina's fate. Many of the French commanders objected to Cesare confining Caterina, arguing that it went against French law. Cesare argued back that as he was the commander of the victorious army, then he had all rights over the prisoner. It was only when money was brought into the equation that the French finally backed down, although Allegre still was not keen on her being placed back into Borgia's hands. But there was little he could do and she once more found herself in Cesare Borgia's clutches with no chance of freedom.

They left Forli the following morning after attending mass in the local Cathedral and hearing the City Elders give oaths of loyalty to Cesare. Forli was well and truly in the hands of the Borgia now, and their once proud leader who had walked the ramparts of their great fortress had come crashing down to earth. They began the long road back to Rome where Caterina would be held as a guest of His Holiness the Pope. But despite having been beaten, Caterina refused to let herself be broken down by the cruelty of the Bull who had finally brought her to heel.

When Cesare arrived in Rome with Caterina Sforza as his hostage, he must have expected her to have been locked up in the dank dungeons of the Castel Sant' Angelo without any thought. Instead, disappointment reigned supreme as she was immediately lodged in the sumptuous Belvedere villa in the gardens of the Vatican. There, although she was a prisoner, Alexander VI allowed her to keep a small number of serving women along with a Florentine priest who acted as her confessor and her confidant. But after a failed escape attempt in May 1500, she was cast into the dungeons of the very fortress that she had once held against the College of Cardinals. She was held captive within the imposing fortress for over a year until, after French demands that she be released, she was allowed her freedom on 30 June 1501. From there, after having agreed to Borgia demands (including reimbursement of the cost of keeping her locked away), she went into a quiet retirement first in Rome and then in Florence where she died following a debilitating illness on 28 May 1509.

Chapter 8

The Duchess and the Devil

Cesare's return to Rome with Caterina Sforza as his hostage was celebrated wildly in the city. The day after his return and public reception, he took part in a huge triumphal procession through the city, the theme of which was the triumph of Caesar. Among the cortege were eleven decorated wagons bearing images of the crossing of the Rubicon – Cesare had crossed his own personal Rubicon in the years since his brother's death, and his victory in the Romagna only made him feel more powerful. Indeed, he would very shortly adopt the motto of *Aut Caesar Aut Nihil* – Either Caesar or Nothing. So triumphant was Cesare was that his father invested him with the titles that had once belonged to his late brother – on 29 March, 1500, Cesare was made Gonfalonier and Captain General of the Church.

But for the moment, Cesare could do little more than wait out the summer. He had achieved so much since throwing off the crimson robes of his Cardinalate and had been kept so busy in furthering his plans, that the days of waiting and watching as things played out in Milan must have been incredibly difficult. He had to watch and wait as the French tried to retake Milan from Ludovico Sforza – indeed, Milan was a key part in Cesare's plans, and Louis *had* to take Milan to be able to help Cesare. If Louis failed in retaking the city, then Cesare's plans would come to nothing. It didn't help that Louis was showing signs of mistrust towards Cesare either – Charlotte d'Albret, Cesare's wife, remained in France despite requests being made that she should join her husband in Italy. Whilst Pope Alexander had raised money to pay for Charlotte's journey, she herself refused on account of her pregnancy. However, it was Louis XII who had forbidden her to leave France.

When Ludovico Sforza was captured by the French on 10 April 1500, Fortuna once again smiled on Cesare Borgia. Sforza was sent to France where he died eight years later, having been kept locked up for the entire time. Still, it now meant that Cesare could once more throw himself into his work. The cities he had his eye on now were Faenza and Rimini, and he knew he had to put heavy diplomatic pressure on both France and Venice. Without the support of those powers, he knew that he wouldn't have a chance of continuing his work in the Romagna. Pressure was placed upon both but Venice was extremely reluctant to let Cesare have his way and grant their permission for his military endeavours. Even Louis was too busy dealing with Pisa on behalf of Florence to pay much attention to Cesare's plans at first. Still, Cesare was so confident that everything was going his way that he allowed himself to enjoy his summer. And in May, he received news that his wife had given birth to a daughter, who had been named Luisa. Alain d'Albret, Cesare's father-in-law, invited him to join his wife in France but at this point in time, Cesare had no wish to leave Italy. He had far too much to do.

He spent much of his time during the summer of 1500 with his mistress, the courtesan Fiametta de' Michelis. Fiametta, known as an 'honest courtesan' rather than a courtesan who sold her wares on the street, was an incredibly learned woman. She spoke Latin and read the classics – she must have been able to sit and discuss such things deeply with Cesare. In between spending time with his mistress, Cesare astounded the people of Rome with his physical feats such as public bullfighting. But just five days after a spectacular bullfight, in which Cesare cut the head off a bull in one single stroke, an accident hit the Vatican which could so easily have ended in tragedy. During a huge storm on 29 June 1500, lightning struck the Vatican, causing one of the chimneys to collapse over the spot where the Pope was sitting. Three people were killed in the accident, but in a twist of fate the Pope survived. The canopy over his Papal throne had somehow managed to stop the rubble from crushing him. He was dragged out, alive but unconscious, from under the rubble and thankfully his injuries were not severe.[1] It must have been a shock to Cesare whose plans, until that moment, had not taken into account the sudden death of his father. It impressed upon him the urgency to secure the Borgia state and the Florentine envoy reported that 'Il Valentino [will arrange] his affairs with Venice by whatever means he can, because if the Pope died he is well aware that he would be in a very exposed position'.[2]

But tragedy would strike again. Just over two weeks after the accident at the Vatican, on 15 July, Lucrezia's husband was crossing the Piazza San Pietro when he was viciously attacked and desperately wounded. Johannes Burchard, the Papal Master of Ceremonies, reported the event in his diary:

> 'On Wednesday, July 15, at about six o clock in the evening, Don Alfonso of Aragon, the Duke of Bisceglie and Donna Lucrezia's husband, was attacked at the top of the steps before the first entrance to St. Peter's Basilica. He was gravely wounded in his head, right arm and leg, whilst his assailants escaped down the steps to join about forty waiting horsemen, with whom they rode out of the city by the Porta Portusa. The duke, badly wounded, was carried to a room in the Torre Borgia, and there was carefully tended to prevent his dying from his injuries.'[3]

Francesco Capello also described the attack, in a letter back to Florence.

> '…And being on the steps of St. Peter's, under the balcony of the benediction, accompanied by only two of his grooms…four men attacked him very well armed and dealt him three blows: one on the head, very deep; and one across the shoulder, either one of which could be mortal; and another small one on the arm: and by what is known the wounds are of a gravity that he will be in need of God's help: and this evening now they have examined his wounds, they say he is very ill.'[4]

Alfonso was taken to a room in the Torre Borgia where he was watched over day and night by Lucrezia and his sister, Sancia. Rumour once more stalked the streets, whispers of who could have been behind the attack on the duke. Dispatches went backwards and forwards and although names were not actually given, it soon became obvious that there was only one name on everyone's lips; Cesare Borgia. The diarist Sanuto recorded on 19 July:

'It is not known who wounded the said Duke, but it is said that it was whoever killed and threw into the Tiber the Duke of Gandia.'[5]

The attack, although it was bungled, could well have been ordered by Cesare. It was well known just how much Cesare had come to distrust his brother-in-law. It can also be said that Cesare was jealous of the close and loving relationship that Alfonso shared with Lucrezia – whilst this jealousy is, of course, no proof of the incest accusations against the siblings it can go some way to explain just one of the many reasons why Cesare would have wanted his brother-in-law out of the way. What seems likely is that the attempt on Alfonso's life was made by a number of members of the Orsini faction – Alfonso had been in league with the Colonna faction, the Orsini's bitterest enemies, after all. Either way, Cesare certainly showed himself as having been willing to be the one behind the attack and reportedly stated the words, 'I did not wound the Duke, but if I had it would have been no less than he deserved!' Willing or not, it must be said that the attack was a messy one. And had Cesare been behind it, as he would show later in his career, he would certainly have made sure that Alfonso did not survive.

Lucrezia and Sancia nursed Alfonso in his chambers within the Torre Borgia, only allowing doctors summoned from Naples to treat him, preparing his food with their own hands out of fear of a poisoning attempt and taking it in shifts to sit with him. Their hard work paid off and around a month later he was almost completely recovered, able to sit up in bed and laugh and joke with his wife and sister. But all of a sudden, the door burst open and the room was taken over by Michelotto – Cesare's manservant. Whilst the accounts differ slightly but it seems clear that Michelotto did indeed enter the room and seize Alfonso. When both Lucrezia and Sancia demanded to know what was going on, he excused himself and stated that he was simply obeying the will of others but if they wished, they could go to the Pope who would be happy to grant Alfonso's release. The two women immediately ran to Pope Alexander, leaving Alfonso behind with Michelotto – they were gone for just a few moments but when they returned they found Alfonso's door guarded, the armed men outside telling them that Alfonso was dead. Both young women were immediately maddened with grief, neither of whom believed Michelotto's overly hasty story that Alfonso had been struck down by a sudden haemorrhage.[6] Why should he have been, after all, when he had been well on the road to recovery? Alfonso had in fact been strangled and in this case there can be no doubt who was behind the attack on Alfonso, Duke of Bisceglie.

Cesare Borgia.

Alfonso's body was taken to the church of Santa Maria della Febbre. But the question remains as to why Cesare would have ordered the murder of his brother in law – his jealousy over his sister cannot have been the only chess piece in play. Rather, politics would have had more of a part to play than anything else. It must be remembered that Cesare, since throwing off his Cardinal's robes, had allied himself entirely with France whereas Alfonso and his entire family were allied with Spain. Cesare had spent a lot of time away from Rome until his return during the Jubilee year of 1500 and it would have been blindingly obvious when he returned that Alfonso and Sancia had pulled his sister into their close knit circle of friends, a close knit circle whose interests were the polar opposite of his own. Cesare had to make sure that everyone within the Borgia circle at the Vatican court walked the same path that he did – his father's political interests, more importantly, had to match his own and given how close Alfonso was to Lucrezia, who Alexander doted upon, Alfonso had to be removed from the equation. It was also no secret

Portrait of a Gentleman by Altobello Melone (c.1513) said to be Cesare Borgia.

Portrait of a Woman by Bartolomeo Veneto (c.1520) said to be Lucrezia Borgia – Städel Museum.

Pope Alexander VI by Cristofano dell Altissimo – Vasari Corridor.

Portrait of a Woman by Innocenzo di Pietro Francucci da Imola (16th Century) possibly Vannozza Cattanei – Galleria Borghese.

Portrait of Cesare Borgia by an
unknown artist – believed to be a
copy of an original by Bartolomeo
Veneto – Museo di Palazzo
Venezia. (*Scan from Uwe Neumahr:*
Cesare Borgia. Der Fürst und die
italienische Renaissance, *Piper,*
München 2007)

Castello Borgia, Nepi. (*Photo by puckillustrations*)

Coat of Arms of Pope Alexander VI adorning the side of the Castel Sant Angelo, Rome. (*Photo by Matthew Bryan*)

Panorama of the Castel Sant Angelo, Rome. (*Photo by Samantha Morris*)

Statue of Pope Alexander VI in
Gandia, Spain. (*Photo by luisfpizarro*)

View of the Castel Sant Angelo from across the Tiber River, Rome. (*Photo by Samantha Morris*)

Borgia Coat of Arms adorning the side of a well in the Courtyard of Pope Alexander VI, Castel Sant Angelo, Rome. (*Photo by Samantha Morris*)

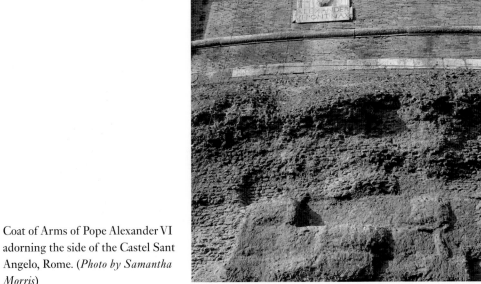

Coat of Arms of Pope Alexander VI adorning the side of the Castel Sant Angelo, Rome. (*Photo by Samantha Morris*)

P.G Spoleto piazza Campello e la Rocca, 1955 – Collezione caroline Albertamos – view of Spoleto Castle.

View of the castle at Spoleto. (*Photo by Jacopoph*)

View of the Pasetto Borgo, the covered walkway connecting the Castel Sant Angelo and the Vatican. (*Photo by Samantha Morris*)

Salita dei Borgia, Rome. This is said to be the last place that Juan Borgia, Duke of Gandia, was seen alive prior to his murder in 1497. (*Photo by Samantha Morris*)

Tower at the top of the Salita dei Borgia, known as the Torre Borgia. (*Photo by anamejia18*)

Salita dei Borgia, Rome. This is said to be the last place that Juan Borgia, Duke of Gandia, was seen alive prior to his murder in 1497. (*Photo by Samantha Morris*)

View of St. Peter's Basilica, Rome. (*Photo by Samantha Morris*)

Gravestone of Vanozza Cattanei, mother of Cesare and Lucrezia Borgia, at the basilica of San Marco, Rome. The tombstone bears the name of her children and was originally located at the place of her burial in the Church of Santa Maria del Popolo, Rome. (*Photo by Samantha Morris*)

Bust of Leonardo da Vinci in the gardens of the Villa Borghese in Rome. (*Photo by Karl Allen Lugmayer*)

The Chateau at Blois, where Cesare married Charlotte d'Albret. (*Photo by Gary*)

Rocca dei Ravaldino at Forli, where Caterina Sforza held out against the army of Cesare Borgia. (*Photo by pacolinus*)

The Castle at Cesena. (*Photo by claudiozacc*)

View of Castillo de Chinchilla, Spain, where Cesare Borgia was imprisoned. (*Photo by JackF*)

Castillo de Chinchilla, Spain, where Cesare Borgia was imprisoned. (*Photo by Héctor S. Marqueño*)

Castle of La Mota, Medina del Campo, Spain. Cesare Borgia spent some time imprisoned here before escaping and fleeing to Navarre. (*Photo by José-Manuel Benito*)

The Church of Santa Maria, Viana, where Cesare Borgia is buried. (*Photo by Stanislava*)

View from the terrace of the Castello Estense, Ferrara. (*Photo by Samantha Morris*)

Tomb of Cesare Borgia. Church of Santa Maria, Viana, Spain. (*Photo by Aleksei8*)

View overlooking Ferrara from the Lion's Tower at the Castello Estensi. (*Photo by Samantha Morris*)

Cathedral of St. George, Ferrara (undergoing renovations in June 2019). (*Photo by Samantha Morris*)

Tomb of Lucrezia Borgia in the Monastery of Corpus Domini, Ferrara. (*Photo by Samantha Morris*)

The Statue of the Archangel Michael atop the Castel Sant Angelo, Rome. (*Photo by Matthew Bryan*)

Interior of the Church of Santa Maria del Popolo, Rome. Juan Borgia was buried here following his murder in 1497, and his mother Vanozza was buried close by. There is no trace nowadays of their final resting place within the Church. (*Photo by Matthew Bryan*)

just how much Lucrezia loved her second husband. Could Cesare have noted this and believed that Alfonso was taking his beloved sister away from him? Cesare was, after all, an incredibly proud young man and any dent to that pride would be met with particular violence. Alfonso of Aragon, Duke of Bisceglie, was a threat not only to Cesare Borgia's political life, but his personal life as well. And he had to be got rid of.

It was not long until an excuse was given as to why Cesare had murdered Alfonso. He stated that Alfonso had tried to murder him by leaning out of a window and shooting at him with a crossbow as he walked in the garden. But whether or not Alexander, who had been visibly shaken and incredibly upset on the attack on Alfonso, believed his son, he certainly made out publicly that he did. Lucrezia was another matter, however. Her grief at the death of her beloved husband was boundless and embarrassed Pope Alexander so much that he sent his daughter away to the castle at Nepi. It should be noted that the day after Alfonso's murder, Cesare visited Lucrezia in her rooms. He was surrounded by a number of armed body guards. But what transpired between the two siblings is not known – did she hate her beloved brother for murdering her husband? Did she forgive him? These are questions questions to which, unfortunately, we will never know the answers, although it is telling that Cesare felt able to visit his sister so soon after the tragic event.

The murder shook Rome to its very core and had the populace terrified of the Borgias, Cesare in particular. He was ruthless and the event had shown just how ready and able he was to get rid of anyone who stood in his way. On 2 October, Cesare left Rome via the Via Flaminia to begin the second phase of his Romagna campaign. As the nobles of Italy quaked in their boots, Cesare marched with his army of 10,000 men towards his next objective.

Chapter 9

The Third Marriage

Whilst Lucrezia was hidden away at Nepi, her father was already contemplating a third marriage for his daughter. But Lucrezia initially opposed another match – her first two marriages had ended in scandal and the people whispered awful things about her. However, she could not stave off being bound in holy matrimony forever and in the September of 1500, she received an offer of marriage from Louis de Ligny, a French nobleman. Lucrezia refused his offer, stating that she did not wish to leave Italy. Further suits followed from Francesco Orsini and Ottaviano Colonna. Still she refused and when the Pope demanded to know her reasons for it, she replied, 'Because my husbands have been very unlucky!'[1]

Thankfully for Cesare and Alexander, Lucrezia soon came around to the idea of another marriage and was particularly taken with the idea of a marriage to Alfonso d'Este. They had set their sights high for the third marriage – the Estes of Ferrara were one of the oldest and grandest families in Italy. In February 1501, Alexander had the Cardinal of Modena write to Ercole, the head of the Este family, proposing an alliance between the two families. Ercole was initially horrified at the idea and tried his best to worm his way out of things – after all Alfonso had previously been married to a princess and it would be unseemly for him to now marry a bastard with a sullied reputation. Ercole, despite being pressed by Alexander, tried desperately to find a French bride for his son – one of the suggested brides for him was the daughter of the Count of Foix, and Ercole urged Louis XII to help him find a suitable bride for his son. When Alexander pressed again, Ercole replied that the marriage of his son was now out of his hands – everything was down to the king of France. It was a clever move from Ercole and Louis was as horrified as Ercole over an Este alliance with the Borgias. There was no advantage to Louis if the marriage went ahead so, when the Ferrarese envoy Cavalleri once more asked the king to help with the marriage issues, the king told him that he was unwise to consider a Borgia alliance and that he would do his utmost to find a French bride for Alfonso. But whilst Ercole pressed Louis, the Pope was also pressing him into getting Ercole to agree to Alfonso marrying Lucrezia. Letters were also sent to Ercole, stressing that the alliance between the two families would mean that Ferrara would have the friendship of Cesare, Duke of Valentinois and thus have his protection also.

Luckily, Louis changed his mind and decided that he now supported the Pope's wishes. Ercole was understandably furious at this news and sent letters to his envoy, practically begging him to ask Louis to change his mind. It fell on deaf ears and, just a few days after the letter was written, Cesare was back in Rome to talk with his father about other ways they could get Ercole to agree to the match. In Ferrara, Ercole was bombarded with messages from Louis, the Pope and Cesare, yet still the patriarch of the Este family refused to budge. More letters were sent by Ercole to the king of France begging him for help but by now Louis was growing tired of it all. He responded to Ercole, saying that if he really didn't want the marriage to go ahead then he should make overly difficult demands on the Pope – Louis' envoy to the Borgias even advised the Ferrarese envoy to have Ercole demand the huge sum of 200,000 ducats, absolution from the Papal census, an estate for his son Ferrante, extra benefices for Cardinal Ippolito and support for regaining lost Ferrarese lands.[2] Ercole, realising that the demands were exceptionally high, finally acquiesced to the Pope's wishes and agreed to offer his son, Alfonso, as a husband to the Pope's daughter.

Negotiations over the dowry began and Alexander wrote to Ercole offering half of what was originally asked for. Eventually all was concluded and the marriage contract was drawn up on 26 August and a proxy wedding was arranged. Celebrations were arranged as soon as news of the marriage went public, with cannon fire from the Castel

Sant' Angelo and constant rounds of dancing and parties. Lucrezia impressed the Ferrarese envoys, particularly when she was so tired out from constant dancing that she became unwell, yet still managed to carry on with all that she needed to do.

Lucrezia was, at this point, understandably worried about what would happen with her young son, Rodrigo. Unfortunately, it had been made very clear by Ercole that the child would not be welcome in Ferrara and it would be incredibly unseemly for his son's bride to show up with a child – she was supposed to show herself as virtuous, after all. She announced that her child would remain in Rome with a yearly revenue of 15,000 ducats.[3]

Despite this, the celebrations continued. And it was during this time that Cesare is said to have thrown a huge party in the Vatican that has become known as the 'Banquet of Chestnuts'. Burchard records the event in his diary, although it must be noted that he is the only witness to the supposed orgy that happened. There are documents, however, attesting that a party did happen on that same night; however, it is not mentioned whether or not it was the orgy of legend. Burchard states:

'On Sunday evening, the last day of October, there took place in the apartments of the Duke Valentino in the Apostolic Palace, a supper, participated in by fifty honest prostitutes of those who are called courtesans. After supper they danced with the servants and others who were there, first clothed, then naked. After supper the lighted candelabra which had been on the table were placed on the floor, and chestnuts thrown among them which the prostitutes had to pick up as they crawled between the candles. The Pope, the Duke and Lucrezia, his sister, were present looking on. At the end they displayed prizes, silk mantles, boots, caps, and other objects which were promised to whomsoever should have made love to those prostitutes the greatest number of times.'[4]

At around the same time, a pamphlet came into Alexander's possession that listed every single dark rumour around the Borgia family, twisting them all into apparent fact. This pamphlet was written by an anonymous source to one Silvio Savelli – Burchard quotes it in his diary and yet it seems to be mentioned nowhere else in primary resources. The letter urges Savelli to consider that Pope Alexander is the 'betrayer of the human race' and then goes on to list every single possible sin that the family has committed.[5] The incest supposedly committed between Lucrezia and her family has a prominent part within this vicious diatribe along with tales of Cesare's murderous exploits. In fact the whole letter is just one libel after another:

> 'His father favours him [Cesare] because he has his own perversity, his own cruelty; it is difficult to say which of these two is the most execrable. The Cardinals see all and keep quiet and flatter and admire the Pope. But all fear him and above all his fratricide son, who from being a Cardinal has made himself into an assassin. He lives like the Turks, surrounded by a flock of prostitutes, guarded by armed soldiers. At his order or decree men are killed, wounded, thrown into the Tiber, poisoned, despoiled of all their possessions…'[6]

Alexander, as was typical of him, found the whole thing rather amusing. Cesare, on the other hand was less than impressed. Since he was a young man he had not dealt well with slights on his pride and, during the December following the Savelli letter, he took action against a masked individual who was wandering the Borgo uttering insults against the Pope's family. The man was seized and had his right hand removed and his tongue cut out. The hand, with its tongue attached morbidly to its little finger, was hung from a window of a nearby Church as a warning to anyone who dared speak out against the Holy family. Similarly, the following January, a Venetian was arrested for daring to translate a libel against Alexander and Cesare. Whilst the Venetian ambassador tried desperately to save the man from his fate, it was all in vain. The man was summarily executed that very same night, and when the Venetian ambassador tried to speak with the Pope about the incident, the Pope simply replied, 'The Duke is good natured, but he has not yet learned to bear insult.'[7]

Lucrezia would soon be leaving Rome forever and in December, news reached the Vatican that her escort had left Ferrara. They arrived on 23 December, met by Cesare, a large escort and a number of Cardinals before being taken to the Vatican to greet Pope Alexander. Lucrezia met her escort the next day, wearing a mulberry gown and a necklace of rubies and pearls. Now, with the escort in Rome, proper celebrations could happen as well as the highly anticipated proxy marriage.

This took place just after Christmas on 30 December. Her escort from Ferrara had brought with them a casket of beautiful gems including the Este family jewels but, unfortunately for Lucrezia, she was only permitted at that point to have access to the wedding ring. She would receive the remaining ornaments following the official marriage, once she reached Ferrara, in case she were to unexpectedly die on the journey. The Este family, who already refused to allow her young son Rodrigo to join her in her new home, did not wish him to inherit any of the gifts that they had given her. This must have been another massive blow to Lucrezia, who was already leaving her son behind forever. Following the ceremony, in which Lucrezia was dressed in a gown of beautiful gold brocade, she stood at a balcony above the Piazza San Pietro and watched as the celebrations for her marriage continued. After watching the festivities which included a mock siege, the wedding party moved to the Borgia family's private apartments where they partied until the early hours of the following morning. There the attendees ate and danced, with Lucrezia dancing with her brother. The piazza outside was cordoned off for bullfights which took place over the next two days whilst in the evenings, the party continued within the Papal apartments.

The celebrations could not last forever, however, and the hour of Lucrezia's departure began to loom. Alexander was understandably distraught at the thought of his beloved daughter leaving Rome and, on the day of her departure, she spent time alone with him before he summoned Cesare to join them. When the time came, she was escorted from Rome by Ippolito d'Este and Cesare in the midst of a thick snowstorm and, as they left, Alexander moved from window to window of the Vatican in order to catch one last, solitary glimpse of his beloved daughter.

Lucrezia's journey northwards took her through her brother's recently conquered states. The journey itself was a slow one, only made slower by the fact that Lucrezia and her women found the wintry conditions incredibly difficult, and Lucrezia's frequent demands for the entire company to stop just so that she could wash her hair. At Spoleto, she made sure that they stopped for an entire day because she and her ladies, made up of her cousin Angela Borgia as well as a number of other young noblewomen, were exhausted from the journey. The Ferrarese envoys sent word ahead to Ercole, Lucrezia's new father-in-law, and warned him of the delay. Yet everywhere Lucrezia went, she and her entourage were greeted with huge amounts of enthusiasm.

On 18 January, Lucrezia and her party made it to Urbino where they were greeted by Elisabetta, the Duchess of Urbino. The duchess, perhaps somewhat awkwardly for Lucrezia, was a relative of her first husband Giovanni Sforza. Yet despite the fact that Elisabetta had very few reasons to love Lucrezia's family, she made sure to greet the newest member of the Este family warmly. The two women even travelled together from Urbino towards Pesaro – for this part of the journey, Pope Alexander had provided his daughter with a magnificent litter so she would not have to struggle through the muddy roads on horseback.

Pesaro, by this point, was in the hands of her brother. But it must have been odd for the young duchess to step foot once more in the town of which she had once been countess. Giovanni Sforza, her first husband, had long been ousted from the town and this time on her arrival, she was greeted by a choir of young children all dressed in the colours of her brother, the Duke of Valentinois, as well as a number of noble ladies who had once been her subjects. Despite the past and the scandal that had existed around the end of her marriage with Giovanni, she was greeted warmly by her former subjects. Following her brief stay in Pesaro, Lucrezia continued on her journey, trailing through the various states of the Romagna – all of which were ruled by her brother. And as Lucrezia passed through each of her brother's domains, the people were ordered to greet her and, at Imola, Lucrezia insisted on stopping the journey to wash her hair. This was something that Lucrezia did often as she was incredibly proud of her long, blonde locks. Maintaining it, therefore, was one of her biggest priorities.

On 29 January, Lucrezia entered Bologna accompanied by Elisabetta. Just outside the city, they had been greeted by members of the Bentivoglio family and as she made her way through the city, the people lauded her entry. On the first evening, a magnificent ball was thrown in her honour and by the end of the evening, Lucrezia was so exhausted that the next morning she slept late and her servants didn't have the heart to wake her.

Following her brief stay at Bologna, Lucrezia rode out to Bentivoglio on 31 January. There she was met by her new husband, Alfonso d'Este. The visit was a surprise one and the two spent some time conversing with each other on various subjects. They then made the joint decision to finish the route to Ferrara by land, as opposed to by water which is how Lucrezia had originally wanted to finish her journey. Alfonso's sudden arrival must have seemed incredibly romantic to Lucrezia, especially from a young man who was not exactly known for his amorous tendencies and it must be noted that up until that point, Alfonso had been less than enthusiastic about marrying her.

Unlike her previous husbands, Alfonso d'Este shied away from usual court life. Rather than enjoying the pomp and circumstance, he preferred to keep to himself and spend his free time in his own personal foundry. On top of that he was an excellent soldier and leader of men. He also enjoyed the company of whores and, like many young men of the age, was scarred from contracting syphilis – so affected by the scars upon his face, he had felt unable to attend the funeral of his first wife who unfortunately lost her life in childbirth. Yet despite this, he was a lover of music and art, patronising such Renaissance greats as Titian.[8]

Following the surprise meeting, despite agreeing with Alfonso to complete the journey by road, Lucrezia and her entourage finalised their trip by travelling the remaining miles to Ferrara by water. She was met by her new sister in law, the formidable Isabella d'Este, at Malalbergo. The relationship between the two women would not be an easy one. Isabella certainly made no secret of her distaste for Lucrezia, making sure that she went out of her way to compete with the young Borgia at every moment she possibly could. More than anything, Isabella was seemingly jealous of Lucrezia and terrified that when Lucrezia became Duchess of Ferrara, she would be outranked. So she did her best to embarrass Lucrezia at every possible opportunity. Yet Lucrezia, bastard daughter of the Spanish Pope, was about to formally marry into one of the oldest Italian families and her life was about to change forever.

Upon arriving in Ferrara, Lucrezia came face to face with her new father-in-law for the first time. Ercole d'Este, a proud ruler, seemed utterly entranced with her to start with and according to one of Isabella's spies held great 'affection and honour for her'.[9] He had even arranged for her rooms within the palace to be completely redecorated.

Lucrezia's formal entry into Ferrara, which would be completed with her official marriage ceremony to Alfonso d'Este, happened on 2 February 1502. Following a procession which wound its ways through the streets of Ferrara, streets that were crammed with people and utterly awash with colour, Lucrezia and Alfonso were finally left alone in each other's company. Their marriage was consummated at least three times, according to one of Isabella's spies yet, at this early point in their marriage, there seemed to be little more between the couple than sexual attraction. What has to be remembered is that this was not a love match – rather both Lucrezia and Alfonso had been forced into the marriage as pieces on a political chessboard. Still, Lucrezia had managed to charm her way into not only Ercole's good graces, but the good graces of the Este courtiers and envoys also. She dazzled everyone who looked her way, as was reported by Cagnolo of Parma in one of his dispatches:

'She is of medium height and slender figure. Her face is long, the nose well defined and beautiful; her hair a bright gold, and her eyes blue; her mouth is somewhat large, the teeth dazzlingly white; her neck white and slender, but at the same time well rounded. She is always cheerful and good-humoured.'[10]

Surely it was only a matter of time until she managed to get into the good books of other members of the Este family, Isabella in particular?

But unfortunately for Lucrezia, that would not prove to be easy. Isabella knew that Lucrezia was outshining her and, used to being the centre of attention, was absolutely furious over the whole thing. She was particularly irate over how long Lucrezia kept her and other members of the Este court waiting each morning. When, the morning after the wedding, Lucrezia failed to appear before noon, Isabella wrote to her husband, Francesco Gonzaga:

'Yesterday we all had to remain in our rooms because Donna Lucrezia takes so long to rise and dress herself. Your Lordship should not envy me for your not being here at this marriage because it is of such a coldness that I envy anyone who remained in Mantua.'[11]

As for the celebrations that surrounded the marriage, Isabella did her very best to make sure that everyone knew just how boring she found it all. Yet, at every turn, Lucrezia outshone her rival – it was reported that Lucrezia was beautifully dressed and Isabella looked frumpy beside her. It cannot have been easy for Isabella, a legitimate Este daughter, to be so outshone by a young woman who she deemed to be her inferior in every single way.

Ercole, however, was still charmed by his daughter-in-law. Once the wedding festivities were over, he took Lucrezia and Isabella with him to a local convent were they met Sister Lucia, a nun who made up part of Ercole's collection of holy women – Lucia had been targeted by Ercole because of her spiritualism and, in particular, the fact that she suffered with the phenomenon of stigmata, an affliction in which wounds appear on the body corresponding to the crucifixion wounds of Jesus Christ. The hands in particular would be affected along with the wrists and feet. The following day he collected Lucrezia again and took her back to see Sister Lucia, as well as a Sister who had previously been an anchoress in Rome.

But the happiness was not to last. Lucrezia was already highly aware that Isabella was constantly spying on her and things were made worse when Ercole dismissed the majority of her Roman serving women and replaced them with locals. She was left with just her cousin, Angela Borgia, and Adriana de Mila, as well as a core staff of around twenty serving men and women. The rest were now made up of men and women handpicked by Ercole – the women that he employed for her were all under eighteen and the daughters of local aristocrats and nobles. It would be Lucrezia's job to teach them how to be a noblewoman, and she would also be on the lookout for suitable husbands for the young women in her charge. Ercole, well known as a tight fisted penny-pincher, also held back a large amount of Lucrezia's allowance money. Pope Alexander had allowed for his daughter to have 12,000 ducats per year out of her dowry money, however, Ercole was only allowing her the sum of 8,000. It caused a huge amount of arguing between Alexander and Ercole whilst Lucrezia, as she had done in the past during difficult moments and would continue to do later in her life, took herself off to the Convent of Corpus Domini in Ferrara. During her time there, whilst the arguments between the two men carried on, Lucrezia began to show the first signs of being pregnant – except this time she was incredibly unwell and had very little appetite – something that was not reported to Alexander VI until 21 April 1502. In the May of that same year, whilst her husband and father in law had gone to visit the French King, she took herself off to the Este retreat at Belriguardo. There, away from constantly being watched and having her every move reported, she found herself somewhere where she could relax and began to enjoy herself amongst her Spanish intimates who had remained with her. Yet still she remained unwell, struggling with her pregnancy. It would certainly not be the last difficult pregnancy that Lucrezia Borgia would go through – it would be a pattern that she would, unfortunately, repeat right up until the end of her life.

In her unwell state, and evidently tired from all of the arguing over her allowance, Lucrezia began to rebel against her father-in-law. When she returned from Belriguardo she deliberately kept the Este patriarch waiting. According to reports from the Este court, she also became difficult towards her Ferrarese household, to the point where four of them begged Ercole to let them leave her service as only Spaniards found favour with their mistress. At this point, Angela Borgia was dangerously unwell and Lucrezia decided to stay in Ferrara to look after her beloved cousin. She took up residence in the Belfiore and she was still in residence when her brother, Cesare, once more began to take Italy by storm.

Chapter 10

Machiavelli's Prince

As Lucrezia was staying in the Belfiore in Ferrara, Cesare was about to make his most daring military move to date. He had previously taken most of the Romagna and now those who were watching his progress carefully believed that he had his sights set on Camerino and Sinigallia – they did not believe that he would try and take Urbino, despite the rumours that the city was next on his list. In Camerino, the ruling Varano family received word of their excommunication due to their failure to pay the Papal census. But with one of Cesare's officers, Vitellozo Vitelli, taking Arezzo on 7 June and then being joined by another of Cesare's captains, Gian Paolo Baglioni, people began to wonder if Cesare's plans would change. Cesare seemed surprised by Vitelli's move on Arezzo and surprised, in particular, by just how successful he had been during the raid, yet he decided to use this success to further his own ends.

Cesare had indeed set his sights on Urbino, yet used his cunning to make sure that no one really knew what he was doing. Guidobaldo de Montefelto, Lord of Urbino, had received a request from Pope Alexander for Cesare and the papal artillery to have free passage through part of his territories. More worrying was when Cesare demanded he provide 1,000 soldiers to help Vitelli at Arezzo. He was somewhat calmed by Cesare's insistence of fraternal love and his promise that Urbino was safe. But on 20 June, whilst he was eating a meal, he received word that 1,000 of Cesare's men were marching south towards the city. He was then surprised even further when he received word that Cesare himself was just twenty miles away, at Cagli, whilst another 1,000 troops were massed on the duchy's northern borders. Guidobaldo was trapped and barely had any time to escape as Cesare and his army fell on Urbino. He fled from the city on the very same night he received word that Urbino was doomed and spent a week trying desperately to avoid Cesare's men, until he managed to reach safety in Mantua. Just a few hours after Guidobaldo's escape, Cesare rode triumphantly into Urbino. In another brilliantly tactical move, he made sure that he sent his Orsini captains to besiege Camerino.

Cesare's excuse for taking Urbino was that Guidobaldo had turned traitor and conspired not only to help Camerino but also to seize the papal artillery as it was transported through his duchy. Guidobaldo, of course, denied all of this.

It was in Urbino that the Florentine envoy, Niccolò Machiavelli, came face to face with Cesare Borgia for the first time. And it was this meeting which would later inspire the Florentine politician to write his treatise, *Il Principe*. Cesare's name had long been known to Machiavelli, who had been following his career with interest. Even before their initial meeting, Machiavelli had been impressed with just how bold Cesare had been, especially when it came to putting pressure on the indecisive Republic of Florence.

It was Cesare himself who requested a meeting with Florentine envoys in order to discuss a new arrangement with them. Niccolò Machiavelli and Piero Soderini, Bishop of Volterra, rode to Urbino and upon their arrival they were immediately taken to meet Cesare. Their mission was to find out exactly what Borgia's plans were and they wanted to delay him enough so that the French troops promised to Florence by Louis XII would arrive. Louis had agreed to protect Florence should Borgia turn on them, and the king himself was starting to mistrust Borgia.

Their meeting ran through the night and the moment Machiavelli and Soderini came face to face with Borgia, he launched into what can only be described as a rant. Machiavelli described Cesare's words in a long letter back to the Signoria of Florence:

'I don't like this government and I cannot trust it. You must change
it and offer guarantees of the observance of what you promise

me…If you don't want me as a friend, you will find out what it is like to have me as your enemy.'[1]

It was certainly a threat and not a thinly veiled one at that. He gave the Florentine government just four days to make their decision. Once the four days were up, Cesare warned, if the Signoria had not come to a decision over what they were doing, he would send 25,000 men to take Florence by force. The number cited was an exaggeration – Machiavelli had discovered that there were actually no more than 16,500 troops stationed in a camp nearby. Still, the number was a threat and Machiavelli set off for Florence at great speed to deliver this ultimatum to the Florentine government.

Yet despite the threats and the rants, Machiavelli only came to admire Borgia more. He was in awe of this young man who had risen to such power from his beginnings in the Church, he was impressed by this man who had turned Fortuna to his own ends.

Talks continued as Machiavelli rode to Florence and part of what was agreed was that Leonardo da Vinci, the Florentine artist and engineer, would come and work for Borgia. He also demanded a condotta from Florence but this was declined by the Signoria. Both Machiavelli and Soderini knew, however, that Cesare Borgia was not actually free to do as he pleased when it came to the Florentine republic. Despite Louis XII's growing mistrust of him, Cesare still had to be careful not to provoke the French king and risk an already unstable alliance. Florence was under the French king's protection and they knew that once Louis heard about what was happening, he would swiftly put a stop to it. They played for time and, after putting off making a formal decision with Cesare's demands, they learned that Louis was sending 6,000 troops to Arezzo in order to restore order to the city and oust Vitelli from his position of power.

Louis' army was making swift progress towards Arezzo and Cesare seemed deflated by this. Although he initially demanded that the Signoria reopen negotiations for his condotta, when he was met by silence he too went quiet. The wind had well and truly been taken out of Cesare Borgia's sails. On 10 July, the Florentine Signoria sent a letter to Cesare that was full of empty words and promises – Soderini, who had been left at Cesare's little court, recorded Cesare's reaction:

> 'I saw him completely change and his first words were: all this is nothing; those men do not want my friendship, not care anything about it; therefore it will be better to remit this negotiation to Our Lord and the King, who will know how to conduct it to my purpose, because I am not a tradesman and I came to you with that freedom that one looks for between good brothers; and to that alliance which I wish to make and your people care nothing for, and want to give me words of the King which I already know, because they know well that for my honour I cannot climb down from the terms for the condotta, and this asking for time is seeking occasion for the new disputes; and they do not wish to give me security but show that they want to deceive me.'[2]

The refusal of Florence to grant Cesare what he wanted caused him to sink into one of his moods. His anger caused Soderini to flee from the camp the following week. But this anger was actually thinly veiled fear – he was standing on a knife edge and his enemies were watching carefully for him to fall off. Not only that, but Louis was on the verge of completely turning on Cesare, and he knew it. Plus, Louis only cared about his campaign for Naples – Cesare was truly at the bottom of the list of things he cared about.

But the collapse of his plans for Florence was not the only problem that Cesare faced. He was beginning to face danger from within his own camp – his captains, all of whom were close allies of the Orsini family, could very easily band together should they wish and take him down. In fact, a group of his captains met around the end of June to discuss Cesare's betrayal in taking Urbino. But Cesare, although growing more and more suspicious of them, had to bite his tongue and play the waiting game. So he held himself back, secreted away in the beautiful palace of the Montefeltro family.

There were many who were upset with Cesare for taking Urbino in such a way. Lucrezia, in particular, had been shocked at the way it had happened. The Montefeltros had, after all, treated her well on her journey towards Ferrara. Isabella d'Este, incredibly politically astute, rather than concentrating on the fact that Cesare had ousted members of her extended family from their home, wrote to her brother in Rome and asked him to intercede with Cesare on her behalf and ask if he would be kind enough to send her a beautiful Cupid statue from the Ducal palace of Urbino. Cesare acquiesced and sent the Cupid to Isabella along with a note explaining that the Cupid was actually the work of the Florentine sculptor Michelangelo, rather than an ancient work as she previously believed. Whilst Isabella was delighted with the gift, her true feelings towards Cesare became clear in a letter that she wrote to her husband following her receipt of the Cupid. She warned her husband:

> 'It is generally believed that His Most Christian Majesty has some understanding with Valentino, so I beg of you to be careful not to use words which may be repeated to him, because in these days we do not know who is to be trusted. There is a report here…that Your Excellency has spoken angry words about Valentino before the Most Christian King and the Pope's servants…and they will doubtless reach the ears of Valentino, who having already shown that he does not scruple to conspire against those of his own blood will, I am certain, not hesitate to plot against your person…it would be perfectly easy to poison Your Excellency.'[3]

Louis entered Milan on 28 July and almost immediately made his displeasure known over Cesare's jaunts in Tuscany. But Cesare was in no mood to try and calm the French king – he was finally away from Urbino and back at his camp in Fermignano where he spent his time relaxing by hunting in the surrounding hills with his leopards. But when Cesare took a fall from his horse during one of his hunting trips, there were those who said it was simply just a ruse so he wouldn't have to crawl back to Louis and explain himself. But Cesare knew, however, that he had to placate the king's displeasure and so, on 15 July, Vitelozzo Vitelli was ordered to withdraw from Tuscany – if he did not obey then Cesare threatened to march on his lands. Vitelli and Gian Paolo Baglione almost immediately withdrew, both inwardly seething over the way Cesare was handling things. But at this point, the two men had no idea what was in store for them.

On 5 August, Cesare finally arrived in Milan to meet the king. The news that he was coming, initially kept secret by Louis until the last possible moment, spread like wildfire and Cesare's enemies were particularly surprised by just how warmly Borgia was greeted by the king, as was described by a member of the Marquis of Mantua's retinue:

'His Most Christian Majesty welcomed and embraced him with great joy and led him to the Castle, where he had him lodge in the chamber nearest his own, and he himself ordered the supper, choosing diverse dishes, and that evening three or four times he went to his room dressed in shirt sleeves, when it was time to go to bed. And he ordered yesterday that he should dress in his own shirts, tunic and robes, for Duke Valentino brought no baggage wagons with him, only horses. In short – he could not have done more for a son or a brother.'[4]

Louis' court was full of Cesare's enemies, however once they realised that Louis actually liked Cesare, they began to disappear from the court. Louis, however, managed to arrange a meeting between Cesare and one of his most vocal critics, Francesco Gonzaga, in order to end their enmity. It seemed to work and the meeting finished in a betrothal between Cesare's young daughter Luisa and Gonzaga's three year old son.

Cesare left Louis' court on 2 September and, after receiving urgent news about the health of his sister, rode for Ferrara. Since falling pregnant Lucrezia's health had taken a turn for the worse and now, in her seventh month, things were turning grave. On 3 September she had begun to suffer from spasms and her doctors feared for her life – she gave birth at this point, but the child was stillborn. When Cesare arrived Lucrezia was too ill to receive him, however the next morning, she had recovered just enough that she received her brother. She was so unwell and at death's door, so her physicians decided that she should be bled. Cesare held her foot as they bled her, and one of the physicians reported to Ercole d'Este:

> 'Today at the twentieth hour we bled Madonna on the right foot. It was exceedingly difficult to accomplish it, and we could not have done it but for the Duke of Romagna, who held her foot. Her Majesty spent two hours with the Duke, who made her laugh and cheered her greatly.'[5]

The next morning her health worsened again and the priest was called to give her the Last Rites. But Cesare decided that, despite the situation, it was time for him to leave his sister. She would never see him again.

Cesare was back in the Romagna by the September of 1502, where he set up his base at Imola and with him was Leonardo da Vinci and Niccolò Machiavelli. It was at his new headquarters that he began to grow more and more suspicious of some of his condottiere captains. In fact, those condottiere, headed by Vitellozo Vitelli, began to discuss whether or not they should turn on their master. In October, a meeting was put together at the Orsini fortress of La Magione – it was attended by Francesco, Duke of Gravina, Paolo Orsini, Gian Paolo Baglione, Oliverotto de Fermo and Vitelozzo Vitelli. During the meeting, it was agreed that Cesare was a huge danger and if they weren't careful, they would be 'devoured by the dragon.'[6] Still, they were wary of actually turning on Cesare Borgia – he was still incredibly powerful and the French king was standing with him. That alliance with France meant that powerful states such as Florence and Venice would not help the conspirators.

On 7 October, the conspiracy took a new turn – a revolt began against Cesare at the fortress of San Leo in Urbino. At the same time, at La Magione, an agreement was reached between the conspirators – they would attack Cesare on two different sides. It was agreed that Bentivoglio would lead an attack from the Romagna, whilst the Orsinis would head an attack from Urbino. Once the attack was successful, it was agreed, Cesare's lands would be split between them.

When Cesare received news of the conspiracy, he reacted incredibly calmly, saying that their rebellion was actually to his advantage. He even laughed to Machiavelli when he read accounts of the conspiracy and even mocked Vitelozzo Vitelli's lack of being able to do anything:

> 'I know them, both themselves and their troops; and Vitelozzo, who enjoys such a reputation. I cannot say I have ever seen him do anything as a valiant man, excusing himself on the ground of the French disease: he is only good at devastating defenceless places, and robbing those who dare not show him their face…'[7]

But still the conspirators feared to directly attack Cesare. Instead, Cesare managed to take back Urbino from the conspirators, and his states in the Romagna remained loyal to him. Yet Cesare refused to be directly drawn onto the field of battle, sending his men and most trusted captains instead. His inactivity was to win the stalemate between the conspirators and the Duke – whilst he remained quiet, French forces were on their way to join him. And the conspirators themselves were starting to drift apart, some of them sending apologies to Cesare for their part in it all and requesting his friendship and forgiveness. It was a move that would end up destroying them. Cesare turned on all of his charm with those who had initially turned against him and ended up pulling Bentivoglio back to his side.

Cesare was now surrounded by those completely loyal to him, as well as a large number of French troops. Many of the conspirators went to Cesare and asked for peace – agreements were signed with Bentivoglio and the Orsini. The agreement was that both sides would end their enmity towards Cesare and in return he would accept them as his allies once more. But it was all a ruse – Cesare was about to completely turn on those condottiere who had betrayed him. Even Machiavelli sensed that something bad was about to happen – where Cesare had once taken the envoy into his confidence, now he went back into his shell.

In December, Cesare and his retinue left Imola and made for Cesena. It was there that Cesare would show just how brutal he could be to those who he believed betrayed him. On 22 December, one of Cesare's most trusted captains was suddenly arrested. Ramiro de Lorqua was a Spaniard who had just returned from Pesaro – his arrest shocked many as they had no idea whatsoever as to why he had been arrested. Three days later, Christmas Day, de Lorqua was executed in the piazza in Cesena and his body was left there with his decapitated head displayed on a lance. Somewhat morbidly, the axe and execution block that had been used were left in the piazza also. But why had this apparently trusted Captain been executed? Cesare had long been losing trust in de Lorqua and he had previously been removed from his place in Cesare's government. Cesare's reasoning for this was that de Lorqua was guilty of corruption, extortion and grain trafficking. But as for the reasoning behind his execution? It was not made clear at all, leaving people to wonder just what exactly had happened. Even Machiavelli was clueless as to why the captain had been made an example of, although rumours began to make themselves known – many whispered that Ramiro de Lorqua had been involved in a conspiracy to kill Cesare. Whether this was true or not is unclear.

The execution of Ramiro de Lorqua was simply the first step in Cesare's elaborate plan to rid himself of his troublesome condottiere. As Cesare remained in Pesaro, one of his problematic condottieri, Oliverotto da Fermo, took the town of Sinigallia in Cesare's name. Borgia was steps ahead however – he had previously sent small bodies of his soldiers towards Sinigallia and ordered them to take different routes, whilst he himself headed there with a small escort. When he heard the news that Fermo had taken the town, he sent orders to him that all of his troops had to withdraw – Cesare's excuse for this was that he needed room to house his own troops, whilst in reality he was making sure that there would be no chance for resistance. Another order sent was that all gates into and out of the city should be locked, except for the one that he himself would be entering through. Then, just south of Fano, he revealed his plans to a few of his most trusted men.

On 30 December, Cesare left Fano and rode towards Sinigallia dressed in full armour and surrounded by armed men dressed in his livery. The Orsini were the first to meet him, followed by Vitelozzo Vitelli. Oliverotto da Fermo was nowhere to be seen, however, so Cesare sent Michelotto off to get him. Even at this point, Cesare did not give away any of his plans to the conspirators. Instead, he received them calmly and with every sign of friendship – they rode together into Sinigallia, eventually being joined by Fermo, chatting like old friends. Little did they know that Cesare's plans for them were about to come to fruition. But as they entered the city, Cesare's cavalry split off and guarded the one single bridge that Cesare would be using to enter. This move cut Fermo's troops off from the Orsini soldiers outside. It was a clever move that started to have alarm bells ringing for the three condottiere – now there were only Cesare's soldiers inside Sinigallia, and a few of Fermo's escort. For all intents and purposes, they were surrounded. But still Cesare kept things cordial. He rode with them towards a house in the town – they tried desperately to take their leave of Cesare before he could make them enter the house but the Duke insisted that they join him, as he wanted to discuss military matters with them. Practically forced into following their leader, they went into the building and entered a small courtyard. Cesare began heading up a flight of stairs before stopping and giving some sort of signal. At that point the three men were arrested.

The next day, New Year's Day 1503, the three men were executed upon Cesare's orders. They were seated – Vitelozzo and Orsini were back to back – and they were garrotted by Michelotto.

Following the executions, Cesare summoned Machiavelli to him and proceeded to brag about his full reasoning for his actions, making out that he had certainly not done it for selfish means but rather for the good of Florence. Cesare wanted, Machiavelli reports:'

To remove the chief enemies of the King of France, of himself and the Florentine Republic...and to eliminate the seeds of trouble and dissention calculated to ruin Italy for which your Lordships ought to be under great obligation to him.'[8]

It was moves like this that enthralled Niccolò Machiavelli, who had been following Cesare on his mission around the Romagna on the orders of the Florentine government, and inspired him to use Cesare as his model for *The Prince*. This was a work of realpolitik in which Machiavelli states that princes and leaders can justify the use of immoral means to achieve their ends. *The Prince*, which was not published until five years after Machiavelli's death in 1532, has one particular chapter in which Machiavelli celebrates Cesare's means. In it he states, without actually mentioning Cesare by name, that:

'There are two ways of fighting: by law or by force. The first way is natural to men, and the second to beasts...so a Prince must understand how to make a nice use of the beast and the man... So, as a prince is forced to know how to act like a beast, he must learn from the fox and the lion; because the lion is defenceless against traps and a fox is defenceless against wolves. Therefore one must be a fox in order to recognise traps, and a lion to frighten off wolves. Those who simply act like lions are stupid. So it follows that a prudent ruler cannot, and must not, honour his word when it places him at a disadvantage, and when the reasons for which he made his promise no longer exist...Men are so simple, and so much creatures of circumstance, that the deceiver will always find someone ready to be deceived.'[9]

It is clear from Cesare's actions that he was capable of playing both the fox and the lion and, whilst Cesare Borgia was certainly not a good man in the modern sense of the term, it was his actions and his brilliance at playing these games that had him being hailed as the most accomplished military leader of his time. He was at the top of his game and had the Romagna well and truly under his thumb. He was a tough but fair ruler, a man who led by fear but kept people who had been unhappy under previous leadership happy.

Unfortunately for Cesare, it was all about to come crashing down.

Chapter 11

The Tide Turns

In Ferrara, Lucrezia had finally been restored to full health following her particularly bad pregnancy and illness. Life was about to get much better for her – Ercole d'Este had finally agreed to grant her the full 12,000 ducats a year from her dowry that Alexander VI had been insisting upon. The miserly Ercole granted her 6,000 ducats for herself and a further 6,000 for clothing and to maintain her household. It was a win for Lucrezia and she set out to enjoy her life at the Este court.

When her husband, Alfonso, and her sister-in-law, Isabella, left Ferrara in the May of 1503, Lucrezia became the centre of attention at court. In fact, because of her, the Este court became full of literary young men with aspiring writers, poets and philosophers flocking to her side. This group included Antonio Tebaldea, Aldus Manutius and Giangiorgio Trissimo, a celebrated humanist scholar. She became particularly close with Ercole Strozzi, a poet who had been born and bred in the city of Ferrara. It was through him that she would meet a gentleman who would become one of her closest friends and confidants – the famous writer and poet Pietro Bembo, a young man who would later come to be thought of as one of Lucrezia's lovers.

The two formally met at a ball in the January of 1503, thrown for her by Ercole Strozzi and Bembo was a well-known face in Ferrara. He had lived there for a number of years whilst his father held the office of co-ruler, after Ferrara lost their war with Venice in 1484. More so, since 1502 he had been staying at the home of Ercole where he had, from time to time, entertained Lucrezia. It was here where the young poet fell head over heels in love with the young Duchess – after one of these meetings, Bembo wrote to Ercole and told him that he had found Lucrezia to be the most beautiful woman he had ever seen, and that he wished she could have stayed longer. It was these visits that inspired Bembo to begin writing poems that would sing Lucrezia's praises. These poems, many of which were written whilst he was away from Ferrara, were sent to members of Lucrezia's inner circle who passed them on to the duchess. Strozzi, aware of Bembo's obvious feelings for Lucrezia, encouraged the two of them and they began to exchange letters and poems – on 25 May 1503, Lucrezia sent a love poem to Bembo, copied from the poet Lope de Estuniga. It may be that Lucrezia was simply just teasing Bembo at this point in their relationship, but it certainly foreshadows just how deep their relationship would go over the following years:

> 'I think were I to die
> And with my wealth of pain
> Cease longing,
> Such great love to deny
> Could make the world remain
> Unloving
> When I consider this,
> Death's long delay is all
> I must desire,
> Since reason tells me bliss
> Is felt by one in thrall
> To such a fire.'[1]

Bembo responded with a poem, written in Tuscan, in which he describes himself as being caught up in her golden hair. The poem was sent to her in a letter on 3 June 1503, along with a book by Gli Asolani:

> 'The glowing hair I love despite my plight
> Since love abounds the more I feel the smart,
> Had slipped the snood which keeps the rarest part
> Of all the gold I crave locked out of sight.'[2]

The letters continue back and forth, full of passion – something which, at this point, Lucrezia was not getting from her husband. In one of the early letters, from June 1503, Lucrezia asks him to help her come up with a motto that she could have inscribed upon a medal. He replied that she should use the Latin words *Est Animum* as 'I can think of giving it no nobler location than the soul'.[3]

It was only after 19 June 1503, that the letters seem to go from platonic to fully, passionate love letters. In a letter dated 19 June, Bembo says that:

> 'Gazing these past days into my crystal, of which we spoke during the last evening I paid my respects to Your Ladyship, I have read therein, glowing at its centre, these lines I now send to you upon this paper. It would be the sweetest consolation to me and more prized than any treasure if in exchange your Ladyship might permit me to see something that she may have read in hers.'[4]

It seems clear from this letter that Pietro Bembo is in love with Lucrezia and that, during a face to face meeting, they exchanged declarations of love. Lucrezia's reply to him clearly mirrors these feelings:

> 'Messer Pietro mio. Concerning the desire you have to hear from me regarding he counterpart of your or our crystal as it may rightly be reputed and termed, I cannot think what else to say or imagine save that it has an extreme affinity of which the like perhaps has never been equalled in any age. And may this suffice. And let it be a gospel everlasting.'[5]

It is evident that things were becoming serious between the couple – Lucrezia even began signing her letters 'ff' rather than her own name. If these letters were to fall into the wrong hands and her name was clearly on the parchment, then things could get very difficult for her. She was, after all, right in the middle of a court in which she was constantly spied and reported upon. At the very least, were this to happen, then Lucrezia's marriage could be annulled on the grounds of adultery.

As summer dawned in 1503, Lucrezia's life was about to change for the worse and she would find herself in an incredibly dangerous political situation.

August, one of the hottest months of the year in Rome, was deadly – malarial fever raged during the summer months and the majority of the College of Cardinals left the city to get to the cleaner air in the country. Previous Popes, including Pius II and Sixtus IV, had died in August and Rodrigo Borgia, Alexander VI, commented that 'This month is fatal for fat men'.[6] Normally, Rodrigo would have followed the example of his Cardinals and left the city for the summer months, however in 1503 he opted to stay, given the tense political situation involving France, Spain and even his own son. It would prove to be his undoing.

One August evening, Alexander and Cesare attended a dinner with the new Cardinal Castellesi – a week later on 12 August, Pope Alexander was struck down with a fit of vomiting and fever. Cesare fell unwell also, however he would later recover. It didn't take long for rumours of poison to spread around the city of Rome and beyond – it was said that Cesare and Alexander had planned to poison the new Cardinal, however, the wine glasses were mixed up, meaning that they poisoned themselves rather than their intended target. The more likely explanation was that both Alexander and Cesare were struck down by the malarial fever that was raging throughout the city. The Pope was bled by his physicians, who took nine ounces of blood – it seemed at that point that the bleeding worked as the fever had lessened. He was bled again on 14 August but the following day he was still running an incredibly high fever and temperature. The envoy Guistiniani reported:

'The fever continues to torment him and there is some danger. I have been told that the Bishop of Venosa says that the Pope's illness is very grave.'[7]

On August 18, Pope Alexander VI died from the fever that he had contracted. Still the rumour of poison persisted, yet he died a completely natural death caused by fever. Yet still the story of poison persists in the Borgia myth – it mixes itself in with the rumour of incest and has made its way into a number of histories and modern day adaptations of the Borgia story. But those who say Alexander and Cesare were poisoned ignore the fact that they had no motive in poisoning Castellesi – he was only newly elected to the Cardinalate and was no threat to them. Not only that, but no poison existed that would take over a week to kill someone.

Although Cesare was dangerously ill at the time of his father's death, he managed to order his men, led by Michelotto, to head to the Papal Apartments and gain access to the Pope's stronghold – the rooms had previously been stripped of almost everything of value by members of the Pope's retinue. Yet Michelotto still managed to pull together over 300,000 ducats worth of cash, silver and jewels. At four o' clock that very same afternoon, Michelotto and his men threw open the doors to the Papal apartments and announced that Rodrigo Borgia, Pope Alexander VI, was dead.

Now, with the Pope dead, Cesare Borgia's life was suddenly in more danger than it ever had been before – although he was still deathly ill, he was about to be thrown headfirst into a political maelstrom. But first the Pope had to be buried and that was the job of Johannes Burchard, the Papal Master of Ceremonies, who had so diligently recorded Alexander's reign. Burchard, who found the Vatican completely deserted as the Cardinals had fled to protect their homes in the rioting that would doubtless ensue, had Alexander's body laid out in the Sala del Papagallo in the Borgia apartments. There Burchard spent the night alone with the crimson robed corpse of his master. The next day, the body was carried to St Peter's basilica, the bier carried by a group of paupers – however fighting broke out inside the ancient church and the guards tried to steal the wax tapers that were being carried by the accompanying monks. The monks fled and in the ensuing chaos, Alexander's body was abandoned.

Johannes Burchard was one of the few who did not forget that they were there to bury the late Pope and dragged the body behind the grille of the High Alter where it would be kept safe from looters while he went off to take care of other business.

Burchard records a rather morbid detail in his diary. When he returned to the basilica later that afternoon, he found the Alexander's body had begun to decompose at an alarming rate:

> 'Already by four o'clock on the afternoon when I saw the corpse again, its face had changed to the colour of mulberry or the blackest cloth and it was covered in blue-black spots. The nose was swollen, the mouth distended where the tongue was doubled over, and the lips seemed to fill everything. The appearance of the face was then far more horrifying than anything that had ever been seen or reported before. Later after five o'clock, the body was carried to the Chapel of Santa Maria della Febbre and placed in its coffin next to the wall in a corner by the altar. Six labourers or porters, making blasphemous jokes about the Pope or in contempt of his corpse, together with two master carpenters, performed this task. The carpenters had made the coffin too narrow and short, and so they placed the Pope's mitre at his side, rolled his body up in an old carpet, and pummelled and pushed it into the coffin with their fists. No wax tapers or lights were used, and no priests or any other persons attended to his body.'[8]

The historian Gucciardini commented on the death of Pope Alexander and it is his words on the death of the Pontiff that have inspired later tales of Satanic worship and pacts with the Devil made before his passing. In reality, Gucciardini simply records the death of the Borgia Pope, who he clearly did not like very much:

> 'All Rome thronged with incredible rejoicing to see the dead body of the Alexander in Saint Peter's, unable to satiate their eyes enough

with seeing spent that serpent who in his boundless ambition and pestiferous perfidy, and with all his examples of horrible cruelty and monstrous sensuality and unheard of avarice, selling without distinction sacred and profane things, had envenomed the entire world.'[9]

Cesare's life was still despaired of and in an effort to save his life, his physicians put him through a brutal regime. One treatment that he was given involved his entire body being submerged in an oil jar filled with ice cold water – this treatment caused Cesare's skin to peel from his body. The historian, Paulo Giovio, heard that he bore the marks of this treatment for the remainder of his days, which disfigured him alongside the recurrence of his syphilis. Another ambassador reported a much more alarming treatment – although how true this is has been disputed – in which a mule was disembowelled and the beasts' entrails placed upon Cesare's naked body.[10]

Although Cesare began to recover, he was still weak and could not stand against the oncoming tempest on his own. He had certainly been planning for his father's death and later reported to Machiavelli that he had prepared for the event and all of the difficulties that would come with it. What he did not bargain for, however, was that at the time of Alexander's passing, he too would be at death's door.

In Rome, as news of the Pope's passing and Cesare's own terrible illness began to spread, the people began to riot. Already, some of the Borgias' greatest enemies were beginning to arrive back in the Eternal City, ready to head into the Conclave that would elect Alexander's successor. The streets were full of rioters who looted the houses of the Cardinals and the deceased Pope and fighting broke out amongst the two largest and most powerful families in the city, the Orsini and the Colonna. All the while the College of Cardinal's worried about trusting the still unwell Cesare. Instead, they took over the fortress of the Castel Sant'Angelo. Yet even from his sickbed, Cesare showed himself as an astute politician and told the Cardinals that he would serve them as Captain of the Papal Armies. The Cardinals met with Agapito da Geraldini, Cesare's trusted advisor, and an agreement was made. He was confirmed as Captain General of the Papal armies and charged with public security until a new Pope was elected but it soon became clear to Cesare that he would not be welcome in Rome during the next Conclave – the Cardinals refused to even enter the Vatican as Cesare lay there in his sick bed, meeting instead at the church of Santa Maria Sopre Minerva – yet still he conspired to make sure that his enemies would also not be in Rome for the election of the new Pope. He ordered some of his troops to travel north to intercept Cardinal Giuliano della Roverre and make sure that he did not reach Rome in time.

Cesare left Rome on 2 September 1503, with an escort of 200 knights. Due to him still being incredibly unwell, he travelled in a litter with the curtains drawn. He was met on the other side of the Tiber by Prospero Colonna – the two men had previously reached an agreement in which they would combine their forces and destroy the Orsini faction. He then slipped away from Colonna and travelled to Nepi, close to where a consignment of French troops were camped.

Giuliano della Roverre had managed to reach Rome in time, despite Cesare's attempts to thwart him and he immediately began to recruit support for the upcoming Conclave whilst others did the same. Cardinal Ascanio Sforza, who had recently been released from captivity by Louis XII, began by supporting della Roverre but soon turned his thoughts to himself. But it was Cesare who had the most to lose in the Conclave – whoever was elected could make or break him. He had on his side eleven Spanish Cardinals who had been ordered to completely shun Giuliano della Roverre. Because of this, during the Conclave, no one Cardinal had enough support to be elected. So they had to come up with a compromise, a man who would not last long as the Pope but who would give the Cardinals enough time to agree on a decent Pope. Thus they elected Francesco Todeschi Piccolomini, a man who was so decrepit that it was clear he would not last long in his new role. Piccolomini took the name of Pius III and his election proved to be incredibly popular with the people of Rome – they were delighted that an Italian had been elected rather than a Frenchman or another Spaniard.

In Nepi, Cesare had lost most of his army. The reason for this was that the French king was utterly disgusted with Pius III's election so ordered that his troops to return to him so they could resume their mission to Naples. Thus Cesare was practically on his own, with only his loyal Michelotto at his side. He sent a message to the new Pope asking if he could return to the Eternal City – he would be safer there, after all. Pius agreed for Cesare to return, making sure that he agreed that he would keep the peace in the Romagna. It seemed in that moment that Pius favoured Cesare – he wrote to the people of the Romagna, asking them to accept Cesare as their lord and gave him the position of Gonfalonier of the Papal armies once more. This must have comforted Cesare who had not so long ago been on the verge of losing everything.

It soon became clear, however, that Rome was not safe. The streets of Rome were in an uproar with Colonna and Orsini soldiers roaming about completely unchecked. Borgia made the decision to move from Rome to Soriano in an effort to stay safe but, before he could leave the city, he and his entourage were headed off by a group of Orsini soldiers and they had to turn back. Instead they went to the Castel Sant' Angelo, making for safety within the fortress by fleeing across the Passeto Borgo. The passeto, which still exists today, is a raised passageway that connects the Vatican to the Castel Sant' Angelo – it was erected by Pope Nicholas III in 1277 and changes have been made to it throughout history. It was used by many Popes in times of danger, including later during the Sack of Rome in 1527.

Pius had been crowned as Pope on 8 October but just ten days later, he was dead. Once more the city was plunged into chaos yet Giuliano della Roverre knew his time had come – he had wanted the Papacy for years and jealousy had clouded his vision when Rodrigo Borgia had been elected over him in 1492. He would make sure that 1503 would his year and almost immediately began working to garner support for his election.

The Conclave began on 1 November and would turn out to be one of the shortest in history. It lasted only a few hours and della Roverre had got his greatest wish – he was now the Pope. The Venetian envoy reported:

> 'No one has any influence over him and he consults few or none. It is almost impossible to describe how strong and violent and difficult he is to manage. In body and soul, he has the nature of a giant. Everything about him is on a magnificent scale, both his undertakings and his passions. He inspires fear rather than hatred, for there is nothing in him that is small or meanly selfish.'[11]

Cesare had no choice now but to support one of his greatest enemies and it was a decision that would prove to be his undoing. Della Roverre's hatred of the Borgia family knew no bounds and he was willing to play Cesare like a fool, assuring him in one moment of their friendship and then the next stabbing him in the back. Following his election as Pope Julius II, he sent assurances to Cesare in the Castel Sant' Angelo that he would be perfectly safe and he was welcome to leave the fortress and move back to the Vatican. Cesare, assuming that Julius was still a man of his word, did just that. He was lodged in a set of apartments with a view towards the rooms that his father had previously occupied – he was now a guest in a palace that had once been his home and he was surrounded by vipers. It seems strange that Cesare would trust a man who for so long had plotted against his family yet there really was not much else he could do. He was backed into a corner and had to make the best of things. And his best bet was to trust the new Pope Julius II, which would prove to be one of the biggest mistakes he would ever make.

Chapter 12

Aut Caesar Aut Nihil

With Cesare being practically imprisoned in the Vatican, Lucrezia was in Ferrara, worried about her brother's future. It was well known how much Pope Julius II despised Cesare and how he was stringing him along. But Lucrezia's worry over her brother's future was causing a rift in her marriage with Alfonso – her husband supported Venice, who were very much against Cesare and his rule in the Romagna. The diarist Sanuto reported that Alfonso complained to the Venetian envoy:

'[The Venetian Signory] do not wish him well and he does not know why if it were not for the men sent by Donna Lucrezia to help Valentino, and he has not given him a penny ... it would be good to act together with Don Alfonso, who wishes evil to Valentino.'[1]

Despite their disagreements over Cesare and his ever worrying situation, Lucrezia spent much of her time pregnant so it seems obvious that Alfonso was at least slightly attracted to his wife. In fact, she would find herself almost constantly pregnant, without much of a break, up until the very end of her life in 1519. Sadly for Lucrezia, she would find many of her pregnancies difficult and many of them would end in stillbirths – towards the end of 1504 she was pregnant again and, sadly, she would miscarry this child in 1505. Yet she still tried desperately to help her brother as his situation was growing more and more precarious – in the final months of 1503, Pope Julius was trying desperately to bring Cesare's states in the Romagna under his own control. In December, Cesare's trusted right hand man, Michelotto de Corella, was captured just outside of Arezzo, an event that pleased Pope Julius to such an extent that he bragged about it to Machiavelli who was currently back in Rome as the Florentine ambassador. Michelotto's capture threw Cesare into a depression and he agreed to hand his Romagnol fortresses over to Pope Julius. But when Julius sent an envoy to one of the Romagnol cities, Cesena, the populace weren't happy with the news that they were now under Papal control and Cesare's lieutenants beat the envoy before hanging him from the castle walls. This, of course, irritated Julius to such an extent that he threw Cesare into the Torre Borgia where he was kept as a prisoner, rather than the 'guest' he had been previously. In an almost vicious twist of irony, the room in which Cesare was detained was the very same room in which Lucrezia's second husband had been strangled on the orders of Cesare. One wonders just what he must have felt at this reversal of fortune.

Cesare's incarceration flung the remaining members of the Borgia faction into a total panic. Gioffre went to Naples along with Cesare's illegitimate children – it is unknown just how many he had, but we can be certain that he had a good number of them. Two of them that we can be sure went to Naples are Gerolamo and his sister Camilla Lucrezia. The mothers of these two children are unknown – whilst Vanozza signed over the deeds of her property to the church of Santa Maria del Popolo.

In early 1504, Cesare was told that he would be free to travel to Naples as long as he handed over the remainder of his fortresses in the Romagna. Cesare agreed and headed to Ostia, where he would take a ship and head for Naples. But once he arrived at Ostia he found himself to be the victim of the sort of double cross he himself had once been able to pull off without a hitch. Gonsalvo de Cordoba, the great Spanish captain, had him arrested on 26 May, just as Cesare was preparing to leave – he was under orders from the Spanish monarchy to have Borgia arrested. They had been convinced by Maria Enriques, Juan Borgia's widow, that Cesare needed to be brought to justice for Juan's murder. And so Cesare found himself promptly shipped off to Spain in fetters. In the space of just a few days, he had lost everything – all of his fortresses in the Romagna were now in the hands of Julius II with the last remaining

Borgia stronghold at Forli handing itself over to Julius just a few days before Cesare was sent to Spain, to be held prisoner in the imposing fortress of Chinchilla, high in the Valencian mountains. His cities were gone, his wealth was gone and now his freedom was gone.

News of Cesare's imprisonment and his being taken to Spain threw his sister into despair. Her anguish drove her father-in-law, Ercole d'Este, to write her a comforting letter – despite how their relationship had started out and his initial refusal to grant her dowry money to her, the letter clearly shows just how much that relationship had changed:

'Be of good heart, for even as we love you sincerely and with every tenderness of heart as our daughter, so we shall never fail him, and we wish to be to him a good father and good brother in everything.'[2]

But there was nothing that Ercole could do. At this point it seemed set in stone that Cesare Borgia would end up locked away for the rest of his life, or at the worst put to death for his supposed crimes. Yet Lucrezia took heart from her father-in-law's letter, as well as news that many other people were demanding that the Spanish Court release Cesare – many of his Spanish Cardinals, as well as his brother in law Jean d'Albret, sent letters to Spain demanding his release. Whilst release did not happen, it seems that they went some way to gaining Cesare better conditions for his confinement – he was allowed eight servants to make his imprisonment more comfortable.

But there was much politicking behind the scenes and there was absolutely no way that Cesare Borgia would be allowed his freedom. Ferdinand and Isabella, were desperate to please Pope Julius II – they wanted him to grant their daughter, Catherine of Aragon, a dispensation to marry her dead husband's brother, the future Henry VIII of England – so they kept him under lock and key. But Ferdinand told one of Cesare's men that he himself had not ordered the arrest of Cesare Borgia, he was simply holding him due to the accusations that had been made against him. At this point, Queen Isabella, was deathly ill with cancer of the womb – it would be up to her, it seemed, to make the final decision on Cesare. But Isabella would never be able to come to a decision as she died on 26 November – this news gave Cesare's supporters hope for his release, although in Ferdinand's mind, his captive could now be used as a political pawn. Rumours abounded in early 1505 that Cesare had been honourably received in Ferdinand's court and Lucrezia received letters seemingly confirming this news. She was, of course, overjoyed. But then definite news was received that he was actually being confined in tighter conditions, thanks to him trying (and failing) to escape confinement.

On 25 October, Cesare tried to let himself down from the small window of the room in which he was held using bedsheets that had been knotted together. Unfortunately for him, his bedsheets broke and he fell to the ground, fracturing his shoulder. He was found there and carried back to his cell where he was kept under much stricter confinement. Another version of the escape story is that Cesare invited the governor of the Castle to join him on the ramparts for a walk. There Cesare attacked him, aiming to throw the governor from the walls to his death, but he was overpowered and taken back to his cell.

Cesare's escape attempt led to him being moved from Chinchilla to the imposing fortress of La Mota, at the Medina del Campo in Castille. Surely Borgia would not attempt to escape from such a place, especially when his cell was high in the tower of La Mota? It was, for all intents and purposes, a maximum security prison and it was deemed to be escape-proof. But the fact that Cesare was kept in such a place did not dampen his spirits – he was soon back to his old games, aiming to take advantage of any political situation he could to gain the freedom that he so desperately wanted.

Cesare soon found himself slap bang in the middle of a political disagreement between Ferdinand of Aragon and his son-in-law, Phillip I, known as the Handsome. Philip wanted to use Cesare for his own ends – in order to take Castille, as well as Naples, for himself – and demanded that he be handed over to him. He would keep Cesare a prisoner until Philip left for Naples, where Cesare would accompany him and help Philip take the city. But Ferdinand refused to hand his prisoner over, stating unequivocally that Cesare must be put on trial for the death of his brother. Cesare watched the argument with a keen eye and soon made up his mind just who he wanted to support – he did not trust Ferdinand and knew that if he remained in his custody, his life would be put at risk. Instead Cesare turned to Philip and, just to be on the safe side, kept in close contact with Jean d'Albret, king of Navarre, his brother-in-law.

The situation was soon to go sour, however. Philip died suddenly on 25 September 1506 thanks to what was described as a chill, although Juana was convinced that he had been poisoned – suddenly the political situation changed at the drop of a hat and Cesare was once more thrown headfirst into danger. A plan was hatched between Cesare and those of the pro-Habsburg party that he had been in touch with, and efforts were made to get Cesare out of the inescapable La Mota.

With Isabella's death, her daughter Juana had been left as the sole heiress to the throne of Spain. The only problem with Juana, however, was that she was completely neurotic and known as '*La Loca*' or 'The Mad' – when her husband died suddenly, she refused to part with his remains even going as far as to travel with his casket across Spain. Philip's death suddenly turned things sour for Cesare. As prisoner in La Mota he would now be fully under the thumb of Ferdinand and his mad daughter – whereas Philip's cause was now taken up by the infant Charles V. It was the Hapsburg faction, working for the young Emperor, who helped Cesare come up with a positively daring plan to escape his prison. The plan was to follow the same lines as his previous escape attempt at Chinchilla except that this time, Cesare had more help – Philip, before his premature death, had managed to make sure that Cesare had a number of servants and a chaplain. It was the chaplain who would provide Cesare with most of the help in executing the escape plot. Borgia had even managed to get his hands on a length of rope, something much hardier than the bedsheets he had tried to use at Chinchilla.

The day set down for the escape was 25 October and at some point during the night, Cesare's chaplain and three other men waited at the bottom of the tower and a rope was let down from the window of Cesare's room. Borgia sent one of his servants down the rope first but unfortunately the rope was too short and the servant fell, injuring himself badly. By this point, as Cesare followed his servant down the rope, the alarm had already been raised and the guards cut the rope from above, sending Cesare tumbling to the ground. The fall injured him and he was helped to a waiting horse by the chaplain but there was no time to help the servant who had fallen first. The young man was found by the guards and summarily executed, on the spot, for his part in the escape.

Cesare and his men managed to escape, riding sixty miles north to the remote castle of Cardenas where he hid away for a month to recover from the injuries sustained in the fall. Once he was well enough to travel, Cesare made for the port of Castres where he boarded a ship that was bound for Navarre, the country ruled by his brother-in-law. Unfortunately, a storm meant that they had to abandon the ship at a remote fishing village where the small party managed to get hold of some mules and they set off the rest of the way to Navarre by land. Then, on 3 December 1506, Cesare appeared at the court of Jean d'Albret, king of Navarre 'like the devil.'[3]

Whilst Cesare began 1505 incarcerated in Spain, the Court of Ferrara was about to be thrown into an uproar. The final months of 1504 had seen the aged Duke Ercole d'Este giving in to the ravages of time – Lucrezia Borgia spent much of her time with her father in law during those last days and, indeed, the two had grown closer despite his initially poor treatment of her at the time of her marriage to Alfonso. Lucrezia, who found out at the end of 1504 that she was pregnant once more, made it her business to comfort the aged Duke as he whiled away the hours waiting for his death.

Ercole died on 25 January 1505 after a fit of fever. It was reported that the Duke died peacefully whilst surrounded by his loved ones –

including Alfonso, who had been travelling to England when news had reached him of his father's illness. Di Prosperi wrote to Isabella d'Este, Marchioness of Mantua, and reported much of her father's last hours as well as passing on his condolences:

'For the one I condole with Your Ladyship and for the other I congratulate you all the more having seen everything come to pass in union, peace and love.'[4]

Although Alfonso was Ercole's heir, the title of Duke did not go to him automatically. Instead, the bells of Ferrara were rung out to convene the Council of the Save, or Council of the Wise, to elect the new Duke. Although the result of this was expected to be a foregone conclusion, reasons of State meant that the Council had to elect a new ruler before the old could be mourned. Alfonso made his way to the Great Hall, dressed in a mantle of white damask lined with squirrel fur and a white hat upon his head. He was then presented with the sword of state and golden rod before being led outside to meet his new subjects.[5] Following Alfonso's triumphal parade throughout the city, he was met at the door of the palace by Lucrezia, who bent down and kissed his hand in a sign of submission to both her Duke and her husband. But Alfonso, in a show of what can only be described as of mutual respect for his wife, lifted her up and kissed her cheek. The two then spent a happy twenty-four hours feasting and celebrating their new positions as Duke and Duchess of Ferrara before the next day the court was plunged into mourning.

The funeral of Ercole d'Este took place two days later and his body was borne through Ferrara to his final resting place in the church of Santa Maria degli Angeli. Upon the body of the Duke was his Order of the Garter, which had been given to him by Edward IV of England, in 1480.[6]

But now, with a new Duke and Duchess of Ferrara, the business of ruling had to take precedence. And one of the first most important bits of business for Alfonso was making sure that both his family and his subjects were secure. Almost immediately, he abolished many of the high taxes that had previously been imposed by his father and made sure to buy enough grain to stave off a famine that was threatening his state. Such moves made him popular with the citizens of Ferrara. He also had extensive work done on the passageway that connected the Palazzo to the Castello, a walkway much like the Pasetto de Borgo in Rome and one through which he had escaped during the rebellion of Niccolo d'Este when he was a child. But this renovation work was for more than just beautification – it connected the palace with Lucrezia's own rooms in the castle, meaning that he could gain access to his wife's chambers in an easier, much more private way. Whilst Alfonso was dealing with such business, Lucrezia took on the entire running of her own household, even going so far as to take over all of the living expenses of those who worked for her. She also showed herself as a woman to be reckoned with, dismissing one of her women for spreading malicious lies and gossip. Yet, despite the change in her circumstances and the love and respect that she and Alfonso had for each other, she continued to exchange passionate letters with Pietro Bembo. Bembo was evidently concerned, now more than ever, that Lucrezia (and ultimately he himself) would be in danger should their letters be intercepted and warned her that there may be spies within her court. Indeed, Lucrezia was watched incredibly closely and her every move was reported to Isabella d'Este.

Lucrezia, despite her happiness at her new position as Duchess of Ferrara, spent much of her time worrying about Cesare as he was kept captive in Spain. She began to work tirelessly in trying to have him released from his imprisonment, even garnering support and help from her husband. Lucrezia and Alfonso wrote to the Ferrarese envoy in Rome, asking him to intercede with the Pope in allowing Cesare his freedom. In August, heavily pregnant, she sent a letter to Francesco Gonzaga once more asking for his help with Cesare, and for him to intercede with the Pope – but her letter was based on pure fantasy and she seemed to completely forget that the current Pope disliked her brother. There was no way on earth that he would allow Cesare to be set free.

On 19 August, in Reggio, Lucrezia gave birth to a son. The child was named Alessandro, after his grandfather Pope Alexander VI. Letters of congratulations poured in, including one from her beloved Pietro Bembo:

> 'It afforded me infinite pleasure to receive in these days the public announcement of the happy birth of a male child to your Ladyship. Especially precious and cheering was it for me since I cannot tell you how anxiously it was awaited in view of the cruel disappointment and vain hopes of last year...As for myself, who have long been a servant to your Ladyship and the Lord Duke, I shall henceforth be more happy in the knowledge that there is born one to whom in due time I shall be able to offer my homage and devotion, and as soon as I am granted the opportunity I shall come to see this sweet little new Lord of mine...'[7]

But Alessandro was a sickly child and died on 16 October, an event which sent Lucrezia spiralling into grief. When Bembo received the news, he wrote to Lucrezia – it would be the last letter she would receive from him for seven years. At this point it has been suggested that Lucrezia had an affair with Francesco Gonzaga, husband of Isabella d'Este. Indeed, she met him as he was en route to Borgorte and she stayed with him there. It has been argued that the affair was completely platonic[8] but whether it was or not, Francesco offered her a space to recover from the birth and quick death of her son, even offering in person to try and help her brother gain his freedom.

Francesco then accompanied her to Mantua where she stayed until the end of October. Whilst there she fanned the flames of rivalry between herself and Isabella d'Este – Francesco was obviously smitten with Lucrezia and Isabella, who was heavily pregnant at the time, could not have been amused at this. Having annoyed her sister-in-law,

Lucrezia left Mantua at the end of October and travelled to Belriguardo where she was met by her husband and, much to her surprise, Giulio, Alfonso's half-brother, previously banished by Alfonso, though the two had since built bridges.

Tragedy was to strike during the stay at Belriguardo, however. Giulio took himself out on a hunting trip and on his way back was met by his half-brother, the Cardinal Ippolito d'Este. Ippolito was in love with Angela Borgia and hugely jealous that Giulio seemed to be getting all of her attention. Angela had scornfully told Ippolito that Giulio's beautiful brown eyes were worth far more than his whole person. Ippolito, fuming at such an insult, ordered his servants to kill Giulio and gouge out his eyes – they promptly obeyed, stabbing Giulio's eyes over and over. Once the deed was done, Ippolito rode back to Belriguardo and informed Alfonso that he had found Giulio lying on the ground – men were dispatched to bring the wounded man back and it was believed he was at death's door or at the very least, that he would be blinded for life. Suspicion, of course, immediately fell on Ippolito but he denied it and said the servants who had committed the deed were not part of his household. Despite knowing the truth, Alfonso was reluctant to have his brother charged, so sent out dispatches saying that Ippolito's version of events was the truth. Ippolito, however, admitted in a letter to Isabella that he had been the one to commit the foul deed. He fled to her court in Mantua but was soon forced to leave. When Giulio began to somewhat recover his sight, Ippolito was granted leave to return where he apologised to his half-brother for his role in the whole affair. But Giulio remained resentful and began to think up all the ways he could exact revenge on Ippolito and Alfonso. Plots were put together with the help of another of his brothers, Ferrante, who was just as resentful towards Alfonso as Giulio was. But whispers of the plots soon began to filter through – knowing that he was on the verge of being caught, Giulio fled to his sister's court in Mantua and when Alfonso ordered Giulio to return to Ferrara, Giulio refused, stating that his life was in danger in his home city. But eventually, Ferrante admitted his part in the plot and betrayed Giulio, telling of how they were plotting Alfonso's assassination. Ferrante was arrested, but Giulio remained in Mantua where he believed he was safe. After a trial on 3 August 1506, both men were found guilty and Giulio was turned over to Alfonso. They were sentenced to life imprisonment. Ferrante died after forty-three years of captivity and Giulio was kept imprisoned for fifty-three years until he was released by his great nephew Duke Alfonso II.

At the end of November 1506, Lucrezia was pregnant again. The news must have been welcome to both her and Alfonso after a difficult year. But in January 1507, she miscarried. Her husband chided her, telling her that she had spent too much time dancing during the Christmas festivities. And to make matters even worse for Lucrezia, her rival Isabella had recently given birth to a son who she, perhaps spitefully, named Ferrante in honour of her imprisoned brother.

1507 would be another year of anguish for Lucrezia Borgia and soon, she would find herself to be a lone Borgia surrounded by wolves.

On 3 December 1506, Cesare arrived in the capital of Navarre, Pamplona, and appeared at the court of his brother-in-law King Jean d'Albret. It was somewhat ironic that the city of Pamplona was the very city that Cesare had been elected as Bishop of back in 1491, and a city that had been up in arms about his elevation to such a high office. Yet now, fifteen years later, they welcomed Cesare Borgia as one of their own. Just days after his arrival, Cesare set about writing to various people of importance in Italy and sending envoys to try and regain some of the power that he had lost with the elevation of Julius II to the Papacy – letters were also sent to his sister as well as to Francesco Gonzaga, which he finalised by signing himself as Duke of the Romagna. Cesare Borgia evidently still had some confidence in his ability to regain his lost land – he was, after all, still popular in the Romagnol cities. Julius II was wise to this however, even going so far as to throw one of Cesare's envoys into prison for even daring to step foot in the city of Bologna.

Cesare had little hope for much support in regaining his old dominions, however. Louis XII of France had stripped him of all his titles and when an envoy was sent to the French King to ask that the Duchy of Valentinois be returned to Cesare, the envoy was met with derision. Louis refused to return the Duchy to Cesare and, in doing so, refused to give him any more of his support. Even Francesco Gonzaga could not be relied on, as he was currently working with Pope Julius II in taming the Romagna. Only Lucrezia seemed to care about her brother's future.

Yet Cesare did not allow this lack of support to get in the way of his plans. He had one goal in mind and that was to return to Italy and regain his land and his power. But unfortunately for him, he still had certain moves he had to make on the political chessboard. One of those moves was to support the young Holy Roman Emperor, Charles V – but before he could put that plan into action he was drawn into a civil war that had broken out between the king of Navarre and one of his captains, Luis de Beaumonte y Luza. Jean of Navarre had ordered Luis to surrender his castle in the small town of Viana, in preparation for expected hostilities between Navarre, France and Spain. But unfortunately for Jean, Luis refused, before beating the royal envoy who had brought the dispatch to a pulp and throwing the poor man into a dungeon. He refused to appear before a court and, after he refused for a third time, Jean declared that enough was enough – Luis de Beaumonte was stripped of his lands and titles and was sentenced to death. Now all Jean had to do was take the castle from Beaumonte before executing him. Cesare was summarily appointed as Captain General of Jean's army and ordered to take Viana from Luis de Beaumonte.

During the first week of March 1507, Cesare and an army of around 5,000 infantry joined up with Jean at Viana. Cesare had led the small army with confidence as they made their way to Viana, making short work of an attack on Larriaga Castle. Italian chroniclers wrote of Cesare's confidence in leading the army in the years following his death, also mentioning that he carried a double pointed lance. This lance was also mentioned by an elderly man who remembered Cesare, who he described as strong and handsome, passing through his village many years previously.[9] The castle of Viana lay just to the east of the town and must have looked like the sort of fortress that would fall to Cesare and his army quickly – it was, after all, not on the same scale as fortresses he had taken whilst he was at the height of his power. But Cesare overestimated his own ability in his planning – previously, he had commanded troops of paid mercenaries but had never had to deal with the sort of weather that battered the town of Viana. Beaumonte's troop were completely hardened to such conditions and on top of that, they were made up of incredibly loyal men. Cesare Borgia would have his work cut out. Little did he know that the events of 11 March 1507, would lead to disaster.

During that night, a vicious storm battered the town of Viana. It was here that Cesare would make his first mistake – he did not believe that Beaumonte would try anything during such horrendous weather and, ever the considerate commander, allowed his men to retire into the town and out of the storm. Beaumont had been watching the town and Cesare's men for such an opportunity and led a convoy into the town, the carts of which were loaded with bread and flour. Once inside the town he sent the convoy on into the castle which they managed to do without anyone noticing. At dawn on 12 March, the soldiers that had been escorting the convoy left the castle – as they began to leave they caught sight of a unit of cavalry heading towards them. Thinking it was the promised reinforcements from Castile, they gave the rallying cry of their leader (Beaumont's) name. Because of this the town flew into a panic and the alarm was raised and Cesare immediately went into action.

He ordered for his squire, a young man named Grascia, to fetch him his light armour as well as a helmet. Once dressed, he leapt onto the back of his steed and galloped from the town with seventy other horsemen behind him. Blinded by his need to take down Beaumonte and win the castle of Viana he had soon outdistanced himself from his men and did not realise that he was now alone.

As he rode out towards the enemy, the lone horseman that was Cesare Borgia was pulled into a fight with three of Beaumont's knights as well as a number of supporting troops. The names of the three knights are known – Garcia de Agreda, Pedro de Allo and Ximenes Garcia. The knights and their soldiers drew Cesare into a ravine where they launched an attack on the lone horseman. As the rain pelted down from the heavens, Ximenes Garcia landed the first blow – Cesare had lifted his arm in order to strike at Garcia, yet his light armour did not protect the area under his arm. Garcia took advantage of this and thrust his lance into the unprotected area. The wound would likely have been a mortal one on its own yet Cesare fought on despite the fact that he was surrounded. He fought for his life until he was completely overwhelmed and fell, only to be stabbed over and over again by his attackers. Twenty five stab wounds later, Cesare Borgia was lying on the rain soaked ground and the man who had once held Italy in the palm of his hand breathed his last. His attackers then stripped him of his armour and left him naked and exposed to the elements. The most they would do for him is place a stone – though some sources say that a flat stone or red tile was used[10] – over his genitals in order to save his dignity in death. Cesare's attackers did not know his identity when they killed him. It was only when Cesare's squire was shown his armour that they realised just who they had killed. The young man broke down when he saw his master's armour and Beaumonte exploded in rage when he was told that Valentino had been killed. His orders had been clear – he had wanted Cesare Borgia to be captured alive. But what was done was done – King Jean approached and Beaumonte retreated so that the King could take possession of Borgia's body. Jean had Cesare's naked body covered with a cloak and then carried into the town of Viana, where he was buried in the little church of Santa Maria – a marble tomb was made for him and inscribed upon it was the epitaph:

'Here in a little earth, lies one whom all did fear; one whose hands dispensed both peace and war. Oh, you that go in search of things deserving praise, if you would praise the worthiest, then let your journey end here, nor trouble to go further.'[11]

The epitaph on the tomb certainly describes Cesare as he was – a man of both peace and war. In his thirty-one years of life he had achieved more than many who lived much longer than him – he had thrown off the crimson of his cardinalate and become one of the most feared warlords in Italy. And in doing that, he had taken the lands of the Romagna, proving himself to be a firm but incredibly fair ruler. Cesare had certainly been feared but he had also been loved and was incredibly popular among the people of the Romagna and its surrounding regions.

Cesare's tomb was destroyed in 1537 and his remains removed from the church by the Bishop of Calahorra, who believed that a godless man such as Cesare Borgia should not be interred in consecrated ground. His skeleton was reinterred outside of the church so that people could walk over his remains. But in 1947, the grave outside the church was reopened and the skeletal remains taken to be examined. The remains, minus the skull which had disintegrated when the grave was originally opened in 1871, were examined by Spanish medical doctor and Cesare Borgia aficionado Victoriano Juaristi Sagarzazu and his colleague Dr Santiago Becerra. Between them they concluded that:

'The general characteristics such as sex, age, height and the stab wound in the left shoulder-blade, made ante-mortem correlate with the circumstances surrounding Cesare Borgia's life and death.'[12]

They also noted further ante-mortem injuries that had them conclude that the remains could only be those of Cesare Borgia – such injuries included one showing that the individual had fallen from a great height and injured their shoulder. Their final conclusion was that there was nothing to say that the skeletal remains found under the pavement were not those of Cesare Borgia. Sagarzuzu worked tirelessly to try and show that Cesare Borgia was not the villain of legend, even designing a monument to him. Unfortunately, this monument was destroyed during the Spanish Civil War and Cesare's remains were not allowed to be reburied within the church of Santa Maria during Sagarzazu's lifetime.

That changed in 2007, however. The Bishop of Pamplona granted his permission for Cesare Borgia to be reburied on consecrated ground within the church of Santa Maria. He was reinterred within the church and today there is only a small plaque upon the church floor to mark his final resting place.

Cesare died alone – and alone was something that he had been for much of his life, although he was surrounded by others. There are those who argue that he went to his death deliberately, or that syphilis had affected his mind to such an extent that he went to his death utterly recklessly. There is a theory that his syphilis would have been completely cured by the malarial fever that he suffered from in 1503, however this is unlikely. The more likely explanation was that at this point Cesare was exhibiting no symptoms of tertiary syphilis as these can take decades to manifest. There is only one mention of his syphilis past this date, in a letter written by Giustinian in 1504. As for him deliberately going to his death, there is nothing to suggest that he would have done such a thing. He had hope, after all, that he would have been able to return to Italy and regain his lands in the Romagna. Instead he went to his death recklessly, with the tunnel vision and single mindedness that he was known for. As such he died violently and he died alone, on the morning of 12 March, just three days short of the Ides of March when his hero, Caesar, had been murdered.

Niccolò Machiavelli wrote of Cesare Borgia's downfall and death in his work of realpolitik, *The Prince*:

> 'So having summed up all that the Duke did, I cannot possibly censure him. Rather, I have been right in putting him forward as an example for all those who have acquired power through good fortune and the arms of others. He was a man of high courage and ambition, and he could not have conducted himself other than the way he did; his plans were frustrated only because Alexander's life was cut short and because of his own sickness.'[13]

Many see Cesare's death as a failure. However, as Machiavelli points out, had Cesare not been sick at the time of his father's death, everything would have been different. Fortuna was against the man who had worshipped her for so long and because of that, Cesare himself was not a failure. He was simply a victim of the fickle goddess.

Chapter 13

'The more I try to submit myself to God, the more he sends to try me'

Lucrezia did not find out what happened to her beloved Cesare for some weeks after his death but on 22 April 1507, Juan Grasica, Cesare's squire who had all but identified the body of his master after the massacre at Viana, arrived in Ferrara. The young man went directly to her brother-in-law, Ippolito d'Este, who could not bring himself to take the news to Lucrezia knowing just how close the siblings had been. Instead, the job of giving her such terrible news fell to Fra Raphael, a friar who was visiting Ferrara that Lent to preach and had spent some time around the Este court.

Upon hearing the news that her beloved brother had been killed, she cried out, 'The more I try to submit myself to God, the more he sends to try me.'[1]Lucrezia was distraught at the news, seeing the death of her brother as yet another tragedy in a very long line of tragedies; every man she had ever loved had died in some awful way – Perotto, Alfonso, her father and now her brother. Yet, just as she had done when she had received news of her father's death, she remained completely stoic whilst in the public gaze. For those looking for a reason to bad mouth the Duchess of Ferrara on account of her grief, Lucrezia Borgia certainly disappointed them. It was only when she was alone in her chambers at night that her ladies could hear her sobbing and crying out her brother's name. Her husband admired the fact that she remained so outwardly calm in the face of such awful news, writing to his brother Ippolito that not only was he grateful for his support, but also that she 'has borne this calamity so patiently.'[2]

She remained in bed for over a month, lost in her grief. When she did finally manage to get herself out of bed, she received Cesare's confidant,

Agapito, who had travelled from Bologna to offer his condolences to the duchess. The two remained locked away for several hours, talking about Cesare. But at this point, Lucrezia was practically alone in her grief. Her husband was away fighting with Louis XII, so she had to deal with her grief almost on her own, with only her cousin, Angela Borgia, to help her come to terms with what had happened. But, seeing just how isolated Lucrezia was, her circle of friends and poets rallied around to help – Ercole Strozzi, a man who had long been in love with the duchess and who had helped to instigate the relationship between Lucrezia and Francesco Gonzaga, wrote a poem about Cesare's passing which he dedicated to Lucrezia. Lucrezia still managed to write daily to her husband, despite her grief, yet in his absence and in her pain she began to seek out solace elsewhere, in the arms of her lover Francesco. The two exchanged coded letters but the situation was made incredibly dangerous given that her husband despised Gonzaga.

By this point, Lucrezia was pregnant again and began to prepare for the carnival of 1508. She made sure that it was a particularly grand affair but it was noted that she did not take part in the dancing towards the end of the carnival – she was heavily pregnant at the time and bed rest was more important than dancing, for the sake of the baby. In March, it was reported that the birth of the child was imminent

She gave birth to the long awaited Este heir on 4 April 1508 and named the child Ercole, in honour of his late grandfather. The child was reportedly incredibly lively and Lucrezia was reported to be doing well after the birth. Yet still she continued to converse with Gonzaga, using Strozzi as the go-between – pseudonyms were of course used in the letters; Alfonso was known as Camillo, Ippolito as Tigrino and Francesco as Guido.[3] But Gonzaga did not return Lucrezia's letters as often as she hoped, perhaps knowing that his relationship with her was more than dangerous, given how much Alfonso disliked him; he used feeling unwell as an excuse not to write which irritated Lucrezia – she wasn't stupid and saw straight through this excuse. Even Strozzi seemed surprised that Gonzaga had not written to her, especially given that Lucrezia was desperate to see him.

After the birth of Ercole, Lucrezia was, unfortunately, too weak to write a letter to her lover in her own hand. Instead she had someone else write it for her and stressed that Gonzaga should come to Ferrara in an effort to reconcile with Alfonso – it would also be a good excuse for her to see him. Yet still Gonzaga used his sickness – probably his syphilis – as an excuse not to leave Mantua.

Despite her happiness at the birth of her son, tragedy was once again about to strike for Lucrezia. After her brother died, Lucrezia took in a Spanish priest, Don Martino, who had accompanied him on his flight from La Mota to Navarre. The priest was given lodgings in the convent of San Paulo and was often invited to court. But on the evening of 4 June 1508, Don Martino was attacked on his way back to the convent from the castle. His throat was slit and he was left to die on the street. Unfortunately, the murderer was never found and the perpetrator of the attack still remains a mystery to this day. Things were only to get worse for Lucrezia – two days later, the body of Ercole Strozzi was found at the corner of Via Praisolo and Via Savonarola. Strozzi's body was covered in twenty-two stab wounds. By his side was his cane and on his feet were his spurs. Tufts of his hair had been pulled out in the struggle and the murderer had arranged them about his head.[4] Whilst Strozzi had not been popular in Ferrara thanks to his harsh ways as a judge, he was famous for his poetry and well known at court. The finding of his corpse threw the town into a frenzy and the question was asked – who killed Ercole Strozzi? But nothing was done to find the perpetrator of the crime.

Rumours, of course, sprang up and legends were born – even years later, the crime was brought up when Pope Julius II openly accused Alfonso of being behind the murder. Other names were mentioned including a man by the name of Masino del Forno, whose method of murder included tearing the hair from his victim's heads.[5] Whoever it may have been, other names included the Bentivoglio family and Galeazzo Sforza, the killer was never found. As well as this we do not know how Lucrezia reacted to the news of Strozzi's death – what we do know, however, is that for some time after the murder she ceased all contact with Francesco Gonzaga. Could she have done this because she felt guilt and shame over having Strozzi act as the go between with herself and Gonzaga, an incredibly dangerous task? However she felt, Lucrezia Borgia never again mentioned Strozzi's name as long as she lived. Just a week after the murder, Lucrezia complained that the weather was far too hot and began talking enthusiastically about taking a trip to the country. At this point she even struck up a friendship with the Queen of Navarre, Isabella of Aragon, who had come to stay in Ferrara after the death of her husband.

Ercole Strozzi had long been the go-between for Lucrezia and Gonzaga, so one would have thought that Strozzi's murder would have calmed her down somewhat. Yet she did not let the tragedy put her off pursuing her relationship with Gonzaga forever. Instead she talked a certain Lorenzo Strozzi, a relation of the late Ercole, into delivering letters that she had written in her own hand – letters that, unlike the previous letters, did not use any sort of pseudonyms whatsoever. It was a dangerous game that Lucrezia was playing here – yet still she wrote ever increasing letters begging to see him, telling him that she would soon be able to visit him in Mantua or even asking him to visit Ferrara. Again Gonzaga wrote telling her that he could not possibly visit her as he was incredibly unwell. But by this point Gonzaga's relationship with Isabella was on the rocks – Lucrezia and Isabella had long been rivals and perhaps their relationship was marred by the love affair. The rift between Francesco and Isabella bled through into the Este family also – Lucrezia and Strozzi of course sided with Francesco on everything, whilst Alfonso and his brothers sided with Isabella. Lucrezia could not, however, stand against her husband – when Isabella demanded that Lucrezia take in a girl who had once resided at her own court in Mantua and who her husband wanted to remain, Alfonso all but forced Lucrezia to write and agree to take the girl in.

Despite the horrors that she faced, Lucrezia was about to enter a period of her life in which, though she would see war, she would triumph. Alfonso found himself almost continually away from home as war took over, leaving Lucrezia to rule Ferrara in his stead.

On 10 December 1508, the League of Cambrai was signed which was, in essence, a peace treaty between Pope Julius II, Louis XII of France, and the Emperor Maximilian in which they would band together against the overbearing might of the Venetian Republic. Venice had scuppered Julius II's plans to have part of the Romagna restored to his rule, and the envoys had faced the Pope with an incredible arrogance. Such behaviour was not to Julius' tastes and so he joined the League, pulling Alfonso d'Este with him – it was a stroke of good luck for Alfonso, who had been at odds with Venice and had failed in his mission to gain peace with the Republic. War was most definitely on the horizon, with Alfonso being made standard bearer of the Church. As such, Ferrara was left in Lucrezia's capable hands. She had, after all, proved herself a competent ruler in the past with her work in the Vatican when her father had gone away, and her work in Spoleto. One of the first acts of war from the League was the Pope's excommunication of Venice. When the Venetian envoys were faced with this news, they simply smiled and sent word to the politicians of Venice, who began to put together their own army against the League. Their army was made up of 50,000 men who were well trained and incredibly well paid.[6]

Despite their numbers, however, the Republic of Venice was soon to realise that going to war with the League of Cambrai without any allies of their own was a foolish endeavour. A huge four day battle began on 14 May 1509 – as the Venetian army was making to move their camp, situated not far from Cremona, the French advance guard came into contact with the Venetian rear guard and decided it was high time to attack. The Venetian army was led by two experienced men, Piero del Monte and Saccoccio da Spoleto and they placed their men in a brilliantly defensive position in a dried up canal bed, well out of the way of the French artillery. However they were soon to make their first mistake – before their own artillery was ready to fire, Spoleto advanced on the French artillery with his militia. The French were ready and attacked their flank with a troop of horse. Venetian losses were huge during the battle and the dead included both Piero del Monte and Saccoccio da Spoleto whilst thousands were slaughtered as they tried to flee. Even the incredibly experienced Bartolomeo d'Alviano was wounded and captured by the French. It was d'Alviano who had led much of the Venetian attack against the French, leading them into an incredibly perilous situation against the French cavalry – as such, he was blamed for the Venetian failure upon the field of battle. Now, a captive of the French king, d'Alviano was sent back to France and when the Venetians asked for his return, they were refused.[7]

The defeat completely demoralised the Venetian army, and following this things were about to get so much worse for Venice. Alfonso d'Este quickly expelled all Venetian diplomats from Ferrara and withdrew his own envoy from Venice. Not only that but thanks to the Venetian loss, Alfonso was able to recover lands that had once belonged to Ferrara. Alfonso's defiance irritated Venice so much that they sent a fleet against him – Alfonso humiliated them. Artillery, positioned cleverly by Cardinal Ippolito d'Este, opened fire on the fleet on 22 December and destroyed six Venetian ships. Nine were then captured whilst only two escaped. It was a humiliating defeat for Venice and it opened the way for a reconciliation with the Pope. They begged for the Pope's forgiveness and in the February of 1510, Pope Julius II lifted the interdict on Venice after it was agreed that Venice would give up their hold on lands around Ferrara.

Unfortunately for Alfonso, Pope Julius decided to turn his ire upon him. Julius greatly resented Alfonso's closeness to the French king and soon, Julius' war efforts would turn upon Ferrara – Julius decided to revert to the policies of his predecessor Alexander VI and once more wanted full dominion over the Papal States, which included Ferrara. He also intended to completely expel the French from Italian soil. In a completely unexpected move, in the early months of 1510, he signed a secret peace agreement with the Republic of Venice and announced that the Duke of Ferrara should be punished for his alliance with France. An attack on Ferrara was imminent. Alfonso tried his best to stop the attack before it could even happen, offering land to the Pope in an effort to appease him. The Pope refused and Alfonso brought in French troops to defend Ferrara. Julius' campaign against Ferrara would last until his death in 1513 and would be taken up by his successor, Leo X. But these were the worst years for Lucrezia and her family in which they saw great danger with Julius moving towards Ferrara, heading much of the attacks on various towns himself – he was known as 'The Warrior Pope' for a reason, after all. He headed attacks on the small towns of Mirandola and Concordia, taking both easily and foiling the French efforts to protect them. These towns were soon taken back by the French, however, and Bologna, which had been in the hands of the Pope, fell to the French in early May. Julius was understandably furious at these losses – they were important in his mission against Ferrara – and on 9 August 1510, an angry Julius placed an interdict over Ferrara. Alfonso and his wife were excommunicated and Alfonso's title was taken from him. In the Pope's eyes, he was no longer Duke of Ferrara and his people were now consigned to the fires of hell.

In a move that cut Lucrezia to the quick, much of the attacks were led by Francesco Gonzaga – he had been captured on 9 August 1509 by the Venetians and imprisoned but Pope Julius had convinced them to release him. Gonzaga was then, in a particularly vicious twist of fate, made Captain General of the Papal Armies whilst his young ten year old son was sent to Rome as a hostage, a promise for his father's good behaviour.

Lucrezia, fearing for herself, her family and her people, wrote to Gonzaga and asked him for his help. The letter was carried to Gonzaga by her ever faithful Lorenzo Strozzi, and she all but begged Gonzaga to look after the interests of her people and to keep their possessions safe. She then asked Venice to provide her and her children with safe conduct towards Parma – it was refused on the basis that they would have to seek the Pope's approval for such a thing. So instead she made ready to leave Ferrara and go to Milan, only to be stopped when her citizens rose up against her and said that if she left, then they would leave en masse. So, for the sake of the people that she so loved, she stayed in Ferrara despite the danger. She did not give in to panic and instead kept calm and collected in a tense situation, even sending spies to Venice – she also wrote a letter to Gonzaga, sent via Strozzi, reminding him of her feelings towards him. Could this have been her way of making him feel guilty for spearheading an attack on her husband and people? Or was it more practical than that – if she reminded him of her feelings for him, then the likelihood of a full blown attack on Ferrara could well be lessened. Around the same sort of time as she wrote the letter to Gonzaga, she received a letter from one of her contacts in Parma, Abraham Thus. The letter itself told Lucrezia of how Modena had been taken by the Pope's forces, but that he himself would work tirelessly to help Ferrara in their own fight against the forces of Rome.

Whilst Lucrezia incessantly wrote letters in an effort to defend her home, the rest of the Este family worked on their own way of defending Ferrara from the forces of Pope Julius II. They stuck together unlike many of those who faced down the Warrior Pope and yet at every turn, Julius tried desperately to drive the family apart – he made out that the Este family had tried to keep Francesco Gonzaga as a prisoner for the longest time and used this to try to drive a wedge between the Estes and Gonzaga. He also managed to get one of Isabella d'Este's greatest enemies right into her court – after all, Gonzaga was working with the Pope so the Este court was the perfect place to put a mole.

Julius made matters even more dangerous in the early months of 1510 when he took himself to Bologna – his main aim for this was to convince Gonzaga to actually join in with his fight to not only regain the Romagna but also in his mission against the Este. However, just as he had done when Lucrezia had tried to convince Gonzaga to visit her, Gonzaga fed Julius the excuse that he was unwell. This time he made the excuse that he was suffering badly with his syphilis. Julius, from his spot in Bologna, watched with glee as the Ferrarese desperately tried to defend itself from any impending attacks. Yet Julius made a serious error in believing that he would easily take Ferrara and its Duchy from the grasp of the Este family – when Julius sent an envoy to Ferrara, demanding the keys to the city, Alfonso took the envoy to see one of his new cannons and stated, to the horror of the envoy, 'These are the keys I would like to give to the Pope.'[8]

All around Ferrara, other towns and principalities fell to the armies of Pope Julius II – worse still, his health had recovered after his recent incident in which he was bed bound with his syphilis, an illness which probably had him feeling sympathetic towards Gonzaga. However, with his health recovered, he reiterated just how much he wanted to take Ferrara and destroy the Este family, commenting to an envoy that he would never give up in his efforts. Lucrezia, however, maintained her calm and instead made sure that life in her court was as exciting as ever – she played host to Gaston de Foix, an exceptional French soldier and nephew of Louis XII, and a number of captains from the French army. Balls and banquets were held in which Lucrezia was praised for her gentle manner. Yet the parties and balls wore her out and on 16 June 1511 it was reported that she had fallen ill. Four days later she had recovered and took herself off to the convent of San Bernadino to convalesce. Yet the treatments that she received there did not work and her illness remained – Alfonso even tried to visit her but was barred from entering given the fact that San Bernadino was a closed convent. Whilst she was there, the French queen expressed a desire to meet Lucrezia, having heard a great deal of her from the French captains. To start with she was so unwell that she was unable to go, her husband even deciding against the trip due to how unwell she was. By early September, Lucrezia was well enough to depart from San Bernadino and travel to Reggio yet she was back in Ferrara by the November whilst the war with Julius II continued to slowly drag on.

In the early months of 1512, Julius II put together yet another League. This one included the usual members of Venice and Spain, but this time also had the indomitable King Henry VIII of England taking part. Alfonso once more went into battle whilst Lucrezia remained at home in Ferrara – on 14 January, at Bastia, he almost lost his life when he was struck in the forehead and returned home so he could recover. It was discovered by the doctors that despite being struck with great force, the bone had not been damaged and he would recover fully. It was certainly a lucky escape for Alfonso d'Este.

One of the bloodiest battles of the wars took place on 11 August 1512 between Alfonso's army and the armies of Pope Julius II. The papal forces, joined by the Spanish, took up positions to the south of Ravenna but they were heavily outnumbered by Alfonso's troops, who were joined by the French army. The Papal forces numbered 20,000 whilst Alfonso's forces, along with the French, numbered 30,000 or more.[9] Not only that but Alfonso had brought his artillery with him. The battle was bloody and ferocious with over 10,000 men being killed, including Gaston de Foix and Cesare's old friend Yves d'Allegre. Prisoners captured included the Papal Legate, Cardinal de'Medici.

Alfonso returned to Ferrara in triumph with his prisoners in tow. But his most eminent prisoners, Fabrizio Colonna and Cardinal de'Medici, were treated like guests rather than the prisoners they actually were. But the victory at Ravenna only saved Ferrara for a short amount of time. The French were completely demoralised following the deaths of their best men and Lucrezia's beloved Francesco Gonzaga tried desperately to calm the Pope, who fell into a rage at the very mention of Alfonso's name, by telling him that Ferrara was already his. It seemed to work and on 11 June 1512 Julius sent a writ of safe conduct to Alfonso, allowing him to travel to Rome in order to submit to him. Alfonso arrived in Rome on 4 July and on 9 July he offered his formal obeisance to the Pope. During the consistory, he kissed the Pope's foot, yet the two still remained incredibly suspicious of one another. When the Pope demanded that Alfonso release his two brothers from their imprisonment, it was unacceptable to Alfonso. Alfonso fled from Rome on 19 July and fled to the Colonna fortress of Marino. He would not reach Ferrara for another three months – his journey was incredibly dangerous as he was followed by the Pope's men who wanted his capture, and spies who reported his every move to Julius.

Alfonso's flight only made Julius more determined to take Ferrara and on 12 August, Lucrezia received a letter from Alfonso who advised her to keep their son Ercole safe at all costs. They could not allow the child to fall into the Pope's hands – the child would act as a hostage in such an event and probably end up being executed. She sent letters to both Isabella d'Este and Francesco Gonzaga regarding her anguish at having to send her son away. Julius had one such letter intercepted and felt so sorry at her sorrow that he wrote a kind letter to her. In a bold move she changed her mind regarding sending her son away from Ferrara, believing that he would be safer with her.

Triumph finally came when, in 1513, Pope Julius died. He had been seriously ill since at least the May of 1512 and passed away due to a fever in the early hours of 21 February 1513. His death brought peace back to Ferrara and, thanks to Lucrezia's work at keeping Ferrara safe and Alfonso's efforts on the battlefield, the couple grew closer. They had a new respect and trust in one another that previously had not been there and in the final years of Lucrezia's life, the relationship between the two grew more ever affectionate – something that Lucrezia had been looking for in a relationship for many years.

Chapter 14

War and Tragedy

Despite the fact that peace had returned to Ferrara, Lucrezia would soon have to deal with yet another personal blow in her life. She was a woman who had been almost constantly pregnant since she had married into the Este family, and had been forced to leave her young son Rodrigo behind when she left Rome for Ferrara. Rodrigo was the son of Lucrezia and her ill-fated second husband, Alfonso of Aragon, and it had been deemed inappropriate for the boy to accompany his mother in her new life. Instead, the child had been sent to an estate in Bari, in Southern Italy, that was run by Isabella d'Aragona, his aunt. There the child had lived in luxury and received rents from tenants in the region whilst his mother sent him clothing appropriate for his rank of Duke of Bisceglie.

But in the August of 1512, Lucrezia received the sad news that her twelve year old son had died. She was, understandably, inconsolable, and retreated in her grief to the convent of San Bernadino and whilst there she lived in complete seclusion for the entire month of September. The first letter that she wrote following Rodrigo's death was on 1 October and she wrote about how completely inconsolable she was.

Other family members were, of course, stricken by the news. Isabella d'Aragona wrote to the governor of Bisceglie – this was not purely a letter to tell the man how she was feeling, but also to compel him to send money that had been owed to little Rodrigo:

'Monsignor Perot: We write this merely to ask you to compel those of Corato to pay us what they have to pay, from the revenue of the illustrious Duke of Bisceglie, our nephew of blessed memory, for shortly a bill will come from the illustrious Duchess of Ferrara, and in case the money is not ready we might be caused great inconvenience. Those of Corato may delay, and we might be compelled to find the money at once. Therefore you must see to it that we are not subjected to any further inconvenience, and that we are paid immediately; for by so doing you will oblige us, and we offer ourselves to your service.

'Isabella of Aragon, Duchess of Milan, alone in misfortune.'[1]

The issue of Rodrigo's inheritance dragged on until 1519, the very year that Lucrezia Borgia died. Following her son's death Lucrezia laid claim to his property and on 9 October she wrote to Francesco Gonzaga to ask him to grant safe conduct to Jacopo de Tebaldi, who she was sending to Bari to deal with her son's affairs and the issue of his inheritance:

'So that I should have those things which duly should come to me and because at present the journey is not safe for any messenger of ours.'[2]

Understandably, Lucrezia was completely bereft at the loss of her beloved son, despite the fact that she had been forced to abandon him upon her move from Rome to Ferrara. Luckily she had company in the form of her brother-in-law, the Cardinal Ippolito d'Este – thankfully he was allowed inside of the convent due to his clerical status, allowing Lucrezia to spend time with someone friendly. However the time he spent with Lucrezia was somewhat sullied by the fact that Alfonso was desperately trying to stay out of the way of the Pope and his spies, sending secret letters to his brother. Isabella d'Este complained bitterly that Ippolito wasn't passing any of the information on to her and did not seem to like the response that she was given – it was too dangerous, in case the letters were intercepted by the Pope's spies. The Pope even tried desperately to bring Francesco Gonzaga, Isabella's husband, on side by promising brilliant promotions for her children as well as reminding Gonzaga that the Este family had long been enemies of the

Gonzaga. The intrigues did not work, however. Instead Francesco and Isabella refused to give in to Pope Julius II, and stood with Lucrezia and Alfonso, despite their own personal enmities.

Amongst all of this, Lucrezia remained closeted behind the walls of the convent where she tried desperately to deal with her grief. She still maintained her correspondence with Francesco Gonzaga whilst her relationship with her sister-in-law, Isabella, remained cold. Lucrezia had left the convent of San Bernadino by 14 August and was back in Ferrara for Alfonso's triumphant return. The two spent many hours in each other's company upon his return, yet the threat of Pope Julius II remained hanging over Alfonso's head like the sword of Damocles. The Pope had taken the majority of Alfonso's lands and, despite the fact that the Ferrarese saw their Duke as a hero for his holding out against Julius, many believed that Ferrara was now on borrowed time. Alfonso decided that because of this he wanted his wife to go to Mantua, where she would be kept safe. Yet Lucrezia had never run away in the face of danger before. Instead she remained in Ferrara and continued to write letters to her beloved Francesco Gonzaga in which she professed her love for him and stated that she would soon visit him in person to tell him just how she felt.

Whilst Lucrezia was enjoying her correspondence with Gonzaga, Gonzaga was having issues with his own wife. Isabella and Gonzaga now led separate lives and the two had not slept together since 1509, thanks to the syphilis that had invaded his body. She kept up her efforts to save her family from the machinations of the Pope, whilst her husband was stuck working for Julius. Isabella desperately wanted him to die, so it would stop the old man's efforts against the Este – she wrote to Ippolito, 'The Pope wants to have all the possessions of the Este in his power, sooner may God ruin him and make him die…'[3]

She would get her wish. His death freed the Este from the threat of war and invasion, and freed Rome from his political machinations. Yet it must be remembered that Pope Julius II did more for the Christian world and the city of Rome than force it into war and politics – it was during his Papacy that the Sistine Chapel was transformed with beautiful frescoes painted by the master artist Michelangelo. He also brought classical statues into the Vatican collection, including the Laocoön group. It was Julius II who also planned for St Peter's to be rebuilt, the plans being entrusted to Bramante who would end up changing the plans dramatically. Julius also had Michelangelo design an opulent tomb for him, which can now be seen in the church of St Peter ad Vincoli. Julius' body, however, is not held within this tomb. Instead he was buried in the new St Peter's, the opulent basilica that he would be remembered for.

Peace had now truly come to Ferrara and one can only imagine the joy that Lucrezia felt over the death of a man who had long been an enemy of the Borgia family. Things were only made better when it became known that a friend of the Este family, Giovanni de'Medici, had been elected as Pope Leo X. Giovanni was the son of the brilliant Lorenzo the Magnificent, a man who had fought against the 'mad monk of Florence' Savonarola, and who had died in the very same year that Rodrigo Borgia had become Pope. It is said that upon his election, Leo stated in a letter to his brother, 'God has given us the Papacy, let us enjoy it.'[4]

Alfonso believed wholeheartedly that the election of Pope Leo X was a good thing for Ferrara and left the city for Rome on 30 March, full of hopes that Leo would absolve him of the accusations made against him by Julius II. He would be bitterly disappointed, however, and it would soon become clear that Leo had intentions for Ferrara that were not friendly. In 1513, Leo put together an alliance between himself, the Holy Roman Emperor, Spain and Henry VIII of England and, in the May of 1513, war broke out again. This time it would last for the remainder of Lucrezia's life, casting a shadow over war weary Ferrara.

Despite the war, Lucrezia kept up her correspondence with Gonzaga. Letters survive from Lucrezia that describe the difficult pregnancies she suffered, such as the one in which she describes the birth of her daughter Leonora on July 4 1515:

'I have been very ill for ten days, very weak and afflicted with complete loss of appetite and with other difficulties but it has pleased God that this evening I was seized by a sudden pain unexpected and unthought of because I thought I had not yet reached my term and gave birth. I am so happy and the little girl to whom I have given birth is well enough…'[5]

The little girl that Lucrezia mentions in her letter would go on to become a nun at the convent of Corpus Domini, the very convent that Lucrezia spent much of her time in during her later years and the convent in which she would be buried. But as was becoming typical for Lucrezia, personal disaster was about to strike with the death of another child. She had given birth to a son, Alessandro, in 1514 yet he was to die in 1516 – an event that would once more send Lucrezia spiralling into grief. On 11 June 1516, Lucrezia wrote a heart breaking letter to Gonzaga, describing her son's death:

'The illustrious Don Alexandro, my last born son, after having been ill for a long time…was forced this past night around the fourth hour to give up his blessed soul to God; which has greatly affected me and has left me in the greatest grief…'[6]

Lucrezia would finally bear a healthy son on 1 November, 1516. The boy was named Francesco and finally, it seemed, Lucrezia and her husband were able to find some happiness. But of course it was short lived. Whilst she was comfortable in Ferrara and the people showed her great esteem, she herself believed that she was never truly loved by the people of her now home. She surrounded herself with her humanist circle, spending her days with poets and highly educated individuals – she encouraged the humanist scholar Aldus Manutius to publish the poems of Tito and Ercole Strozzi, a volume which he dedicated to the Duchess of Ferrara. She also spent her time favouring those in her court with links to Spain – she was desperate to have some sort of link to her family's homeland. Gifts were given to many Spaniards including the Chevalier of Santa Cruz, and she kept as many Spaniards in her circle as she possibly could. Her estate at Belriguardo also became an escape for her and her inner circle – the estate consisted of a large manor house surrounded by sprawling gardens which must have provided a place of calm for a woman so affected in her life by tragedy.

In the January of 1517 Lucrezia received the news that her younger brother, Gioffre, had died at the age of just thirty-six. She was now the sole remaining child of Rodrigo Borgia and Vanozza Cattanei – and not even a year later, Vanozza herself also died. She was buried in the church of Santa Maria del Popolo in Rome, beneath a stone marker bearing the names of all of her children. The grave marker was later removed, leaving no trace of the Borgias who were buried in the little basilica – today the stone is kept in the entrance to the little church of San Marco, next to the Palazzo Venezia, so whilst there is no trace of her left in the place where she was buried, her grave marker has been kept safe for those who know where to look.

Chapter 15

Endings

Lucrezia Borgia had lived a life full of both excitement and grief but, as Carnivale began in 1518, she cannot have known that she had little more than a year left to live. But whilst the people of Ferrara celebrated Carnivale, the court kept to a Lenten way of life and ate frugally – even Lucrezia, who had been unwell with a fever, took part in Lent. Meanwhile, Alfonso had begun renovating the castle, employing artists to repaint the rooms and installing marble facades throughout the building. Lucrezia also commissioned a number of artworks, most of which had religion as their main subjects such as a work by Fra Bartolomeo of the 'Head of the Saviour'. Religion had become increasingly important to Lucrezia and, as well as commissioning religious works of art, she spent much of her time sequestered away in her beloved convents and speaking with her confessor. She also continued corresponding with her sister in law, Isabella d'Este. The two had long had a tough relationship, however their enmity seems to have calmed somewhat by 1518 – Lucrezia wrote to Isabella thanking her for a recipe that Isabella had sent, in the hopes that it would help Lucrezia recover from an illness that had once again kept her isolated.

Despite her ill health, Lucrezia spent much of her time caring for the remaining Borgia children that were in her care – Girolamo Borgia, Cesare's son, and Giovanni Borgia, her supposed half-brother and the infamous '*Infans Romanus*', remained in her care and at the court of the Este. Giovanni was a nuisance, however. The boy preferred the Spanish way of life, insisting on signing himself as 'Juan de Borja' and was a notorious trouble maker. His household was full of rowdy servants and more than once they were involved in fights in the streets of Ferrara. But when a squire was killed by one of Giovanni's men, things took a turn for the worst. Alfonso was furious with the boy and sent him away to Rome and then the French court, in the hope that he would learn some self-control. Giovanni learned no such thing, however. He accepted gifts from the French king and queen yet showed little gratitude and was unable to show any sort of gallantry towards anyone at the court. It did not take long for the French court to grow tired of the witless and ungallant young man – he returned to Italy, yet never set foot in Ferrara upon his return, avoiding the town even after Lucrezia's death in 1519. He eventually sought refuge within the Church, following a lawsuit in 1548 in which a woman accused him of owing her money. Giovanni Borgia, the *Infans Romanus*, around who rumours of being born out of incest swirled, ended his life in the safety of the Church, working as a Papal functionary.[1]

Lucrezia was once more left in charge of Ferrara in the May of 1518, when Alfonso went to take the waters at Abano. During this time, Lucrezia truly showed just how merciful she was – a group of men were arrested for walking about the streets of Ferrara during the night without a light; Alfonso wrote to Lucrezia from Abano demanding that they be tortured for their crime. Instead she refused to torture them and wrote to her husband explaining her actions, telling him that she let them go with a security of 200 ducats.[2]

Illness stalked Lucrezia during these times. She was unwell during May and spent a few days locked in her rooms – though the nature of her illness was not known – and she was unwell again during August. Prosperi reported on her illness, but made no mention of what it was, only that it was her usual indisposition. What could this illness have been? There is every possibility that it may have been syphilis – her husband was known for indiscretions after all, and the disease was so widespread at this time that there is little doubt she would have caught it. There is also the fact that she went through a number of miscarriages, which was a key symptom of syphilis in women. As well as this, the infection may well have been passed on to any living children.

She still worked hard, looking after Ferrara despite being unwell, as well as entertaining Alfonso's gentlemen and men of the court when her husband was away. He had left Ferrara in the November of 1518 in order to try and regain his territories of Modena and Reggio, leaving Lucrezia in charge of the city. Pope Leo X had promised to give Alfonso those territories back for a total of 40,000 ducats and the whole thing had been agreed and signed for in a document drawn up in Ferrara in 1516, and Alfonso's claim was backed both by Francis I of France and Henry VIII of England. However nothing came of it and Leo had decided that he would marry his nephew, Lorenzo de'Medici, to a French princess and give him Ferrara as a wedding gift. Alfonso, of course, could not countenance this and left for France to meet with the French king. Lucrezia, left in charge, was obviously concerned over her husband's safety and wrote to Pope Leo to try and avert any suspicion that he may have held over Alfonso's trip to France. And it was only shortly after Alfonso left that Lucrezia received news of her mother's death.

She was kept informed of her husband's progress in France and was pleased when he arrived safely in Paris, writing to him of her delight over how well he had been received at the French court and sending him news of their children. She even shared the wonderful news with Isabella d'Este. His visit lasted until the early months of 1519 and he returned home on 20 February, heading straight to see his wife where he received joyous news.

Lucrezia Borgia, Duchess of Ferrara, was pregnant again. It was a pregnancy that would be the most difficult of Lucrezia's life, and a pregnancy that would ultimately cause her end.

Francesco Gonzaga, Lucrezia's beloved, died on 29 March 1519, from the syphilis that had wracked his body. Lucrezia had kept up her correspondence with him until the end of his life and, with his passing, wrote a letter of condolence to his wife and her sister in law, Isabella d'Este:

'Illustrious Lady, Sister-in-law, and Most Honoured Sister: The great loss by death of your Excellency's husband, of blessed memory, has caused me such profound grief, that instead of being able to offer consolation I myself am in need of it. I sympathise with your Excellency in this loss, and I cannot tell you how grieved and depressed I am, but, as it has occurred and it has pleased our Lord so to do, we must acquiesce in his will. Therefore I beg and urge your Majesty to bear up under this misfortune as befits your position, and I know that you will do so. I will at present merely add that I commend myself and offer my services to you at all times.

'Your Sister-in-Law Lucretia, Duchess of Ferrara.

'Ferrara, the last of March, 1519.'[3]

On 14 June 1519, Lucrezia Borgia gave birth to a baby girl. The birth was a difficult one and the child was born so weak that it was feared she would not survive long – Alfonso made sure to have the child baptised straight away and named her Isabella. Following the birth, Lucrezia suffered with a mild fever but, given that she had come through difficult pregnancies and fevers previously, it was hoped that she would come through this one. Unfortunately the fever got worse and by 20 June it was feared that she would die. Following the birth, Lucrezia had not been purged of the bad material that had accumulated in her womb – a Renaissance belief that during pregnancy, menstrual blood would accumulate and needed to be purged following a birth. Doctors bled her and, as her head ached, her beautiful blonde hair was shorn off – her nose then bled and she soon became completely incapable of speech and could not see, her illness having struck her with temporary blindness. The doctors gave her just hours to live but still Lucrezia fought – she was a Borgia after all – she woke and regained her senses with Alfonso at her side. Continuing to improve, the doctors said that if she did not relapse then there was hope of her survival.

But Lucrezia Borgia knew she was dying and, using the last of her remaining strength, dictated a letter to be given to Pope Leo X. It is the last letter written by Lucrezia:

'Most Holy Father and Honoured Master,

'With all respect I kiss your Holiness' feet and commend myself in all humility to your holy mercy. Having suffered for more than two months, early on the morning of the 14th of the present, as it pleased God, I gave birth to a daughter, and hoped then to find relief from my sufferings, but I did not, and shall be compelled to pay my debt to nature. So great is the favour which our merciful Creator has shown me, that I approach the end of my life with pleasure, knowing that in a few hours, after receiving for the last time all the holy sacraments of the Church, I shall be released. Having arrived at this moment, I desire as a Christian, although I am a sinner, to ask your Holiness, in your mercy, to give me all possible spiritual consolation and your Holiness' blessing for my soul. Therefore I offer myself to you in all humility and commend my husband and my children, all of whom are your servants, to your Holiness' mercy. In Ferrara, June 22, 1519, at the fourteenth hour.

'Your Holiness' humble servant,
'Lucrezia d'Este.'[4]

The letter to the Pope shows just how heavily the past weighed on Lucrezia and she wanted desperately to receive forgiveness from the highest religious authority in the world as well as to ensure that her husband and children would be looked after.

Still she clung to life and her doctors tried desperately to purge her of the bad material that they believed had accumulated in her womb. Nothing worked however and Ferrara prepared for the death of their Duchess – Alfonso stayed constantly by her side, only moving to eat and sleep a little.

She passed in the fifth hour of the morning of 24 June 1519, unable to fight the fever and sickness that had plagued her not only following the birth of her daughter, but during the pregnancy also, at the age of thirty-nine. Alfonso was utterly grief stricken by her death – he wrote personal letters to two of his friends describing his anguish and that, 'I cannot write without tears'.[5] The two had grown closer during Lucrezia's last years and had a deep respect for each other, even if they did not love one another. She had borne him multiple children, having been almost constantly pregnant since their marriage in 1502, providing him heirs that would rule Ferrara for centuries to come. Not only that, but she was a respected Duchess and the people of Ferrara loved and respected her, deeply mourning her loss.

Lucrezia Borgia, Duchess of Ferrara, was buried in her beloved convent of Corpus Domini where she still lies to this day. Her life had been one of incredible wealth and incredible loss, as well as surviving the terrible rumours that stalked her throughout her life. She was vilified as an incestuous harlot who poisoned her enemies yet the truth was that she was a simple, pious woman who loved her family deeply. Her only crime was to be born a Borgia, their name and actions both real and imagined, tainting her even after death.

Chapter 16

Cesare and Lucrezia in Modern Day Media

'Only a Borgia can truly love a Borgia'

The above quote, from Showtime's *The Borgias* is one that in the modern day many associate with the Borgia name. The quote is associated with the rumour of incest – something that has haunted Cesare and Lucrezia Borgia since long before their deaths. And unfortunately, despite the work of historians, the idea of incest still clings to the Borgia name. In modern day media, the idea of incest is one that is constantly brought up and many media platforms – television, film, novels and video games – make out that the idea of incest and murder are fact.

Television and film are probably the most common medium in which people will first come across the name of Borgia. Whilst such media can be a good way to help an individual gain interest in the period in question, it must be remembered that the stories told in television and film are heavily dramatized and often not as historically accurate as they can be. Take for instance the two main television series based on the Borgia family – Showtime's *The Borgias* and Canal +'s *Borgia*; Showtime's version of the show tells the story of the Borgia's rise to power and concentrates mainly on the relationship between Cesare and Lucrezia. From the very beginning of the first episode, the viewer can see the spark between the two siblings – it starts as playful yet develops throughout the three seasons into a sexual relationship. When comparing the two modern day television shows, there are some huge differences between the two, and one of them has become ingrained within the public mind-set with the belief that the events shown are indeed historical fact. Showtime's *The Borgias*, to those who don't know the Renaissance era, is a good solid piece of entertainment with its high budget, lavish costumes and all-star cast. But if you look beyond the veil of beautiful sets and incredible acting, there are some glaring historical errors – and not all of them are based on Cesare himself.

For instance the show often shows a view of the Dome of St Peter's – this did not exist at the time of the Borgias. Rather, the first plans came into existence in 1506, and the dome wasn't completed until 1590. Glossing over this, however, *The Borgias* also showed Cesare stabbing his own brother and throwing his body into the Tiber, Lucrezia Borgia resorting to poisoning and the death of her second husband at the hands of both Cesare and his sister. Add this on to the incestuous overtures of the show and you have a drama that has sprung from the rumour and propaganda that swept Rome at the time of the Borgia family.

On the other hand, Canal +'s version, *Borgia*, is much more historically accurate – the Vatican is modelled on the old St Peter's basilica and you clearly see Cesare's transformation from Cardinal to soldier. In this version, Cesare, played by Mark Ryder, and Lucrezia, played by Isolda Dychauk, never cross the line and sleep together. It is clear that the siblings were close, perhaps closer than we in this age believe that siblings should be, and the series clearly shows how the rumours of incest begin. Cesare even says in the final episode of season 1: 'The whole world believes we are lovers. Perhaps we should prove them right.' But before any lines can be crossed, the two are interrupted by Lucrezia's lover, Perotto, who is hiding behind the curtains.

Borgia remains true to the history of Cesare Borgia in many ways. Throughout the three seasons, Cesare truly becomes the warlord that history says he was. Juan's death was orchestrated by an unknown assailant rather than his own brother and the Siege of Forli, unlike in *The Borgias*, was done correctly. Although there were some historical inaccuracies, as is to be expected in any historical drama, *Borgia* draws on the historical fact rather than latching onto rumours and twisting them to sex up a script. It must be said, though, that *The Borgias* was far more popular than *Borgia*. This is simply because the general public prefer a sexed up version of history. The stories shown in the Showtime version are a twisted version of history, based solely on rumour and propaganda.

Another series which again shows a skewed version of the Borgia family is the BBC's 1981 series, *The Borgias* which was also turned into a novel by the historian Sarah Bradford. This series was certainly not as historically inaccurate as the later television series of the same name, however there are moments within the series which do insinuate incest – whilst there is little to suggest in this adaptation that Cesare and Lucrezia were involved sexually, there are several scenes of a sexual nature between Lucrezia and her father. This can, of course, be linked to the rumour that was started by Giovanni Sforza during the annulment proceeding between himself and Lucrezia, in which he stated that the Pope only wanted the divorce so he could keep his daughter all to himself.

A particularly good piece of film on the general story of the Borgia family, in particular the story of the two siblings, is the Spanish film *Los Borgia*. The film, starring Sergio Peris-Mencheta as Cesare and Maria Valverde as Lucrezia, is entirely in Spanish and tells the story of the Borgias' rise to power, finishing at the moment of Cesare's death. This adaptation is far more accurate than any other television series or film, and the only mention of incest within it involves simply that it was nothing more than rumour. Rather the facts are stuck to as much as possible, even going as far as showing that Juan Borgia's murder had little, if anything, to do with his brother and the correct way that Alfonso Duke of Bisceglie lost his life. Of course, as with any dramatization, there are certain parts that have been twisted to suit the story – although the creators of *Los Borgia* have done their best to keep these as close to historically accurate, or based on the generally accepted history as possible. One such instance is the mask that Cesare wears at the end of the film. It has long been rumoured that Cesare Borgia was so inflicted with syphilis that towards the end of his life he wore a mask to disguise the scarring upon his face. However it has since been argued that Cesare wore a mask in public so that he would not be recognised – he often preferred his secrecy over being recognised in public, after all. However compared to the blatant inaccuracies and peddling of vicious rumour that is pertinent in many adaptations, this can be seen as little more than a minor inconvenience.

Another particularly good example is *Prince of Foxes,* released in 1949 and starring Orson Welles as Cesare Borgia and Tyrone Power as Andrea Orsini. The piece is an adaptation of a novel of the same name and tells the story of a supposedly loyal servant of Cesare turning on him and refusing to orchestrate the murder of the Lord of Citta del Monte. This servant, Orsini, grows to admire the noble Lord and ends up helping him defend the town against Borgia. The characterisation of Borgia in this film is truly excellent and Welles' outstanding performance truly captures the cold ruthlessness of the man, as well as his military genius. As well as this, there is no mention whatsoever of incest or poisoning and whilst the script paints Cesare as the villain of the piece, it cannot be denied that it truly captures what many must have felt about him as he took over the various cities within the Romagna.

Second to television and film, there are a number of novels based on the life and times of the Borgia family. As with many other media, there are those which are far more accurate than others – despite being fictitious accounts of these people's lives – and those which pander to the rumours that have surrounded the Borgia siblings for centuries. Probably the best, and most accurate, novels written about the Borgia family are *Blood and Beauty* and *In the Name of the Family,* both by Sarah Dunant. Both of these novels have been incredibly well researched and, unlike with many other novels, the relationship between Cesare and Lucrezia is not the be all and end all of the story. Instead, the narrative of both books concentrate on the family as a whole, their rise to power and eventual downfall. The first novel, *Blood and Beauty* tells the tale of Rodrigo's rise to power, the early marriages of Lucrezia and Cesare's rising from Cardinal to soldier whilst the second novel, *In the Name of the Family,* concentrates on what can only be described as the family's downfall. We see the luck of the family changing – Rodrigo's death and Cesare's fall from grace, amidst the amazing things that Cesare did whilst working as a soldier. Much of the story is told through the eyes of Niccolò Machiavelli who spent much of his time with Cesare in his later years. The story itself finishes with Machiavelli reflecting on the death of his one-time friend and the strength of Lucrezia who, at that point was Duchess of Ferrara and still had six years to live. There are, of course, elements of total fiction within the narrative of both novels and Dunant makes a point of mentioning these in the Afterword at the end of the book. She admits that the majority of the mistakes in historiography are indeed deliberate but apologises for those that are not. This is the sort of transparency that an historical novelist should aspire to, and Dunant can only be praised for not only this but her excellent retelling of the Borgia stories.

However for every well written and well researched novel that tells the tale of both the Borgia siblings and their family, there is one that seems to have been written without any thought to the historical fact whatsoever. Many of these tales include incest as the central theme, followed by intrigue and murder. Two such examples of this include *The Borgia Bride* by Jean Kalogridis and *The Vatican Princess* by C.W. Gortner. Incest and sexual intrigue are key plot points in both of these novels, and neither author makes any hint that these plot points are little more than spurious rumour. In fact there is one particular scene in Gortner's *The Vatican Princess* that truly does turn the stomach and involves Juan Borgia, Duke of Gandia, committing the most atrocious rape on his sister, Lucrezia. The example of poison can be found in many novels also – Derek Wilson's *The Borgia Chalice* uses the idea of a chalice that was used by the Borgia family to poison their enemies and, in the story, the same chalice is used to commit murder in the modern day.

A further medium that has been used to introduce the Borgia family is that of video games. Two examples spring to mind here – Assassins Creed

2 and its follow up, Assassins Creed: Brotherhood. Both of these games tell the story of a man named Ezio Auditore who makes it his mission to hunt down those who murdered his parents. This leads to him joining the Assassins and, in his hunt for the murderers he comes across the Borgia family. The Borgia siblings do not play a part in Assassins Creed 2, however their father, Rodrigo, is one of the main antagonists of the game. Cesare and Lucrezia feature prominently, however, in Assassins Creed: Brotherhood. Cesare is the main antagonist of the game and as the game progresses the player sees the relationship between him and his sister. The idea of incest features prominently in this game and the player sees the siblings kiss, whilst Cesare promises Lucrezia that she will be 'his Queen'. Again, as with many examples in both film and the written word, these games make use of the rumours that surround the family – the creators of the game do make it clear, however, that the game is a fictitious work based on historical individuals. That being said, although it introduces the family to its players and can encourage them to read about the real history behind the characters, it has made players believe that what they see in the game is true, thus continuing the thought that the Borgia family were corrupt, incestuous individuals.

But now, as throughout history, people love a good gossip. They want stories of political intrigue and forbidden love, stories that both disgust them and draw them in. It is because of this that modern day adaptations of the Borgia history draw on the rumours that sparked during the Renaissance and use them to their advantage. Despite the fact that these rumours are simply just that, rumours, they do make for some spectacular viewing both on the pages of novels and on the television.

Would Cesare and Lucrezia Borgia approve of the fact that their names have lived on in such a way? Today, despite the efforts of historians, Cesare is still seen as an evil man who slept with his sister. It is forgotten that he unified the Romagna, albeit using some cruel acts, and that under his rule the cities he had taken over prospered. The behaviour that both he and his family exhibited was completely normal – they were people of their time. It is forgotten that Lucrezia was loved by her people and was an incredibly pious woman right up until the end of her life – she was certainly not an incestuous, poisoning harlot. Murder and political intrigue was something that every single noble family took part in. Yet due to the fact that the Borgia family were in a position of power and that they were Spaniards, these behaviours were taken and twisted into something more simply to show them as evil.

Unfortunately for them, despite the efforts of many to rehabilitate them and thanks to the continued vilification through the public medium of books, plays and television, the idea of the Borgia family being the most evil family in history will never truly go away.

Chapter 17

Epilogue

Whilst her brother's bones rested in far away Viana, Lucrezia was buried in her beloved convent of Corpus Domini and today she rests with the remains of her husband, two of their children and Alfonso's mother. They lie beneath a simple marble slab bearing their names. Resting in the tombs nearby them are the bodies of their eldest son Duke Ercole II and his daughter. The body of Eleanora d'Este, Lucrezia's only surviving daughter, also rests in a tomb close by. She became a nun in the very same convent and was an accomplished musician. Her music has recently been rediscovered and both published and performed by Musica Secreta & the Celestial Sirens in the album *Lucrezia Borgia's Daughter*.

But in 1570, an earthquake all but destroyed Ferrara leaving the city to be rebuilt by Lucrezia's grandson, Alfonso II. He was the last legitimate child of Alfonso and Lucrezia to rule Ferrara and, when he died in 1597 much of Ferrara still lay in ruins. It would never again be the beautiful Renaissance city that Lucrezia had known and, later, a Papal Legate would remove Alfonso's remaining treasures from the city taking them all back to Rome. During the reign of Pope Clement VII, the City finally fell to the Papal armies and the glory of the Este was stamped out. Where previous Popes such as Julius II had failed, Clement succeeded.

Both Cesare and Lucrezia left behind their children. Where Cesare left behind only one legitimate child and multiple illegitimate children, Lucrezia's surviving children were all legitimate. Cesare's legitimate child by his wife, Charlotte d'Albret, was named Luisa and never once met her father. Despite having never set eyes on his little girl, during his life Cesare had worked hard to try and find a marriage for Luisa that would take her places and enhance her station in life. These efforts came to nothing, however. She was just fourteen when her mother died and she was sent to be tutored by Louise of Savoy, who would become mother to the future Francis I. In 1517, she married Louis de la Tremouille but was widowed in 1525 when her husband was killed at the Battle of Pavia fighting for Charles V. Five years later, she married Phillipe de Bourbon and by him she had six children. It is thanks to Luisa that direct descendants of Cesare Borgia, the Bourbon Counts of Busset and Chalus, still exist today. Luisa lived until the age of 53, dying in 1553, and signed herself as Louise de Valentinois until her very last moments. Cesare's two illegitimate children who were recorded were named Girolamo and Camilla Lucrezia – Camilla was brought up in Ferrara at the Convent of Corpo di Christo and under the protection of her aunt. She became a nun at that same convent in 1516 and took the name Suor Lucrezia, later becoming abbess of the convent and dying there in 1573. Girolamo was also brought up in Ferrara and placed under the tutelage of an eminent scholar. He married a daughter of the lord of Capri in 1537 and by her had two daughters, who he named after his Este aunts. But whereas his sister had a sweet temperament, Girolamo inherited his father's darker side, nursing long vendettas and committing brutal murders where he saw fit.

Lucrezia's children were all legitimate and it was the birth of Ercole, the Este heir, in 1508 that truly established her position as Duchess of Ferrara. Other children followed but many of them did not survive. Eleonora, who would go on to become a nun in Corpus Domini, would be her only surviving daughter.

The name Borgia continued on long past the deaths of Cesare and Lucrezia and one of the members of the family went a long way in helping to negate the image of the family as complete social degenerates. His name was Francis Borgia and he was the grandson of Juan Borgia, Cesare's brother who was viciously murdered in 1497. More importantly, Francis was the only Borgia family member to be canonised. Francis Borgia was born in 1510 in Gandia, Spain, to Juan Borgia the 3rd Duke of Gandia and Juana, the daughter of the Archbishop of Zaragoza. For the first ten years of his life, Francis remained in Gandia before he was sent away to the court of Charles V, Holy Roman Emperor, in order for him to learn the ways of the noble class; he was, after all, the heir to Gandia, although he would have rather become a monk than the ruler of a Duchy. He married a Portuguese noblewoman in 1529 and then, when his father died in 1543, became the 4th Duke of Gandia. His time as Duke of Gandia, however, only lasted for three years – when his wife died in 1546, he renounced the claim to his title and joined the Society of Jesus, more commonly known as the Jesuits, where he lived a humble life. In 1565, he became Vicar General of the Jesuit order and, using his new position, founded colleges as well as working with popes and kings. All throughout his time in the Jesuits, he refused to have his portrait painted and it was only when Francis was dying that his fellow brothers managed to get an artist into the same room as him. A quick sketch was made of Francis as he slept but that was all the artist had time to do before he woke up and rolled over to hide his face. On the night of 30 September 1572, one of the brothers tried to get Francis to drink some soup but Borgia only managed a small mouthful. He died at a little after midnight on 1 October 1572 and in 1671 was canonized by Pope Clement XI for his pious life and great works.

Few traces of the family remain in Rome, unless you know where to look. One can visit the Borgia apartments at the Vatican and see the beautiful frescoes of Pinturicchio, frescoes which show the images not only of Cesare and Lucrezia but of other family members also. Rodrigo Borgia, Pope Alexander VI, is shown as is Giulia Farnese, his mistress. The Salita dei Borgia at the foot of the church of San Pietro in Vincoli still exists and is said to be the last place where Juan Borgia was seen alive before his brutal murder in 1497. Vanozza Cattanei's Inn on the Campo dei Fiore still exists also, with its Borgia coat of arms on the side of the building. If you look closely enough around the city of Rome, you can notice bits and pieces of Borgia history – from neighbourhoods and churches that the family would have known, to coats of arms plastered on the side of buildings and monuments. Whilst the city as the family had known it has changed considerably, one can still feel the ghosts of the Borgia and their contemporaries stalking the streets of the Eternal City.

Whilst Cesare and Lucrezia Borgia spent much of their lives apart, the two were incredibly close to one another. It cannot be denied that the Borgia family was a devoted one, however they were stalked by vicious rumours both during their lives and after – even after Lucrezia died in 1519, enemies of the Borgia still whispered the poisonous rumours of incest that have come down to us centuries later and woven their way into the public's 'knowledge' of the Borgia siblings. Even in death, with Cesare buried in Viana and Lucrezia buried in Ferrara, the siblings' names have always been spoken together. You cannot have one without the other and, indeed, their story is not complete without telling both sides.

It is unfortunate that, despite the work of many historians such as Sarah Bradford, Raphael Sabatini and Michael Mallet, that public opinion still tars the name of Borgia with the brush of corruption, incest and murder. Even with the work of historians who have worked to clear their names and show them as people of their time, many television series, movies and novels still show Cesare and Lucrezia as in an incestuous relationship, as corrupt and murderous.

It is my hope that with this piece of work I have managed to show that there is more to the lives of the Borgia siblings than what has filtered down into public opinion. Whilst Cesare Borgia certainly committed murder, much of what he did was done in an effort to begin a kingdom in Italy and make sure that the family could hold on to power. Unfortunately, his efforts came to naught – the death of his father in 1503 and the rise of Pope Julius II certainly saw to that. As for Lucrezia, she was the furthest thing from the poisoning harlot that enemies of the Borgia made her out to be. Rather she was a political pawn and a pious woman who suffered far too much. In fact, the real story of history's most notorious siblings is far more interesting than any fictionalised account based on nothing but rumour.

Bibliography

Bellonci, Maria, translated Wall, B., *The Life and Times of Lucrezia Borgia*, Weidenfeld & Nicholson 1953.

Bembo, P., (1515) *Gli Asolani di Messer Pietro Bembo 1515*.

Bradford, Sarah, *Cesare Borgia: His Life & Times*, Weidenfeld & Nicholson 1976.

Bradford, Sarah, *Lucrezia Borgia: Life, Love and Death in Renaissance Italy*, Penguin 2005.

Burchard, J., *Diarium sive Rerum Urbanarum Commentarii (1483–1506) Tome Second (1492–1499)*, Ernest Leroux 1884.

Chamberlin, E.R., *Cesare Borgia*, International Profiles 1969.

Chamberlin, R., *The Bad Popes*, Sutton 2003.

Cloulas, Ivan, translated Roberts, G., *The Borgias*, Franklin Watts 1989.

Cruz, S.M., *Victoriano Juaristi Sagarzazu (1880–1949) El Ansia de Saber: Datos Para una Biografía*, Gobierno de Navarra 2007.

de Roo, P., *Material for a History of Pope Alexander VI, His Relatives and His Time Vol. I*, Bruges 1924.

Ferrara, Orestres, translated Sheed F.J., *The Borgia Pope: Alexander the Sixth*, Sheed & Ward 1942.

Frieda, L., *The Deadly Sisterhood: A Story of Women, Power and Intrigue in the Italian Renaissance*, Weidenfeld & Nicholson 2012.

Gardner, E.G., *Dukes & Poets in Ferrara*, Archibald Constable & Co 1904.

Giovio, P., *Delle Istorie Del Suo Tempo di mons Paolo Giovo da Como, Vescovo di Nocera: Prima Parte*, Venetia 1608.

Greenblatt, S., *The Swerve: How the Renaissance Began*, Vintage 2011.

Gregorovius, Ferdinand, translated Garner, J.L., *Lucretia Borgia: According to Original Documents and Correspondence of her Day*, Appleton & Co 1904.

Hare, C., *The Most Illustrious Ladies of the Italian Renaissance*, Harper & Brothers 1904.

Hibbert, C., *The Borgias and their Enemies: 1431–1519*, Mariner 2009.

Hollingsworth, M., *Patronage in Renaissance Italy*, John Murray 1994.

Hollingsworth, M., *The Borgias: History's Most Notorious Dynasty*, Quercus 2011.

Infessura, S., *Diario della Citta di Roma di Stefano Infessura: Vol. Unico*, Palazzo Madama 1980.

Johnson, M., *The Borgias,* Macdonald 1981.

Laurencin, Marques de, *Relacion Los Festines que se Celebraron en el Vaticano con Motivo de las Bodas de Lucrecia Borgia con Don Alonso de Aragon,* La Real Academia de la Historia: Madrid 1916.

Le Queux, W., *The Closed Book: Concerning the Secret of the Borgias,* Smart Set Publishing 1904.

Machiavelli, Niccolò, translated Bull, G., *The Prince,* Penguin Classics 2003.

Machiavelli, Niccolò, translated Detmold, C.E.,*The Historical, Political and Diplomatic Writings of Niccolo Machiavelli,* James R. Osgood & Co 1882.

Machiavelli, Niccolò, translated Gilbert, F., *History of Florence and of the Affairs of Italy: From the Earliest Times to the Death of Lorenzo the Magnificent,* Harper Torchbooks 1960.

Mallet, M., *The Borgias,* Academy Chicago 1987.

Mallett, M. & Shaw, C., *The Italian Wars: 1494–1559,* Routledge 2014.

Martines, L., *Scourge and Fire: Savonarola and Renaissance Italy,* Pimlico 2007.

Mathew A.H., (trans) *The Diary of John Burchard of Strasburg AD1483–1506: Vols I, II and III* Francis Griffiths 1910.

Meyer, G.J., *The Borgias: The Hidden History,* Bantam 2014.

Miron, E.L., *Duchess Derelict: A Study of the Life and Times of Charlotte D'Albret, Duchesse de Valentinois,* Stanley Paul & Co 1911.

Morris, S., *Cesare Borgia in a Nutshell,* MadeGlobal 2016.

Morris, S., *Girolamo Savonarola: The Renaissance Preacher,* MadeGlobal 2017.

Noel, G., *The Renaissance Popes: Culture, Power and the Making of the Borgia Myth,* Constable 2006.

Norwich, John Julius, *The Pope: A History,* Vintage 2012.

Oppenheimer, P., *Machiavelli: A Life Beyond Ideology,* Continuum 2011.

Sabatini, R., *The Life of Cesare Borgia,* Stanley Paul & Co 1925.

Sanuto, M., *Diarii de Marino Sanuto: Vol I,* F. Visentini 1903.

Sanuto, M., *Diarii de Marino Sanuto: Vol II,* F. Visentini 1903.

Sanuto, M., *Diarii de Marino Sanuto: Vol III,* F. Visentini 1903.

Seward, D., *The Burning of the Vanities: Savonarola and the Borgia Pope,* Sutton 2006.

Shankland, H, (trans, *The Prettiest Love Letters in the World: Letters Between Lucrezia Borgia and Pietro Bembo 1503 to 1519,* Collins Harvill 1987.

Strathern, P., *The Artist, the Philosopher and the Warrior,* Vintage 2010.

Symonds, J.A., *Renaissance in Italy: The Age of the Despots,* Smith, Elder & Co 1912.

Unger, M.J., *Machiavelli: A Biography,* Simon & Schuster 2011.

Woodward, W.H., *Cesare Borgia: A Biography,* Chapman & Hall 1913.

Yeo, M., *The Greatest of the Borgias,* Sheed & Ward 1936.

Yriarte, Charles, translated Stirling, W., *Cesare Borgia,* Aldus 1947.

Notes

Chapter 1

1. Mary Hollingsworth., *The Borgias: History's Most Notorious Dynasty* (Quercus 2011), p. 14; Meyer, G.J., *The Borgias: The Hidden History* (Bantam 2013), p. 29.
2. Karl Kup., *Ulrich Von Richental's Chroncle of the Council of Constance* (New York Public Library 1936), p. 16.
3. Stephen Greenblatt, *The Swerve: How The Renaissance Began* (Vintage 2012), p. 164.
4. Ibid., p. 168.
5. John Julius Norwich., *The Popes: A History* (Vintage 2012), p. 227.
6. Hollingsworth., 2011, p. 16; Meyer, 2012, p. 22.
7. Norwich., 2012, p. 230.
8. Ibid., p. 231; Meyer, 2013 p. 25.
9. Will Durant., *The Renaissance: A History of Civilization in Italy from 1304–1576AD* (Simon & Schuster 1952), p. 350.
10. Christopher Hibbert., *The Borgias And Their Enemies* (Mariner 2009), p. 8.
11. Ibid., p. 14; Ivan Cloulas, *The Borgias (Franklin Watts* 1989), p. 25.
12. Cloulas., 1989, p. 27.
13. Meyer, 2013, p. 36.
14. Norwich., 2012, p. 242.
15. Cloulas., 1989, p. 33.
16. Meyer, 2013, p. 101; Orestres Ferrara, *The Borgia Pope* (Sheed and Ward 1942), p. 56 Ivan Cloulas., 1989, p. 37.
17. Cloulas., 1989, p. 43.

Chapter 2

1. Sarah Bradford., *Cesare Borgia: His Life and Times* (Weidenfeld & Nicholson, 1976), p. 16; Sarah Bradford., *Lucrezia Borgia: Life Love and Death in Renaissance Italy* (Penguin, 2005), p. 15.
2. Leonie Frieda, *The Deadly Sisterhood* (Weidenfeld & Nicholson, 2012), p. 154; Bradford, 1976; Cloulas., 1989, p. 52.
3. Bradford, 1976, pp. 20–21.
4. *Ibid*, p. 19.
5. Paul Oppenheimer, *Machiavelli: A Life Beyond Ideology* (Continuum, 2011) p. 151; trans. Christian E. Detmold, *Historical, Political and Diplomatic Writings of Niccolo Machiavelli (Vol III)* (Boston: James R. Osgood & Company, 1891) p. 269.
6. Peter de Roo, *Material for a History of Pope Alexander VI: His Relatives and His Time* (Bruges 1924) p. 420.
7. *Ibid*, p. 461.
8. *Ibid*, p. 474.
9. *Ibid*, p. 424.
10. Meyer, 2013, p. 242.

11. Michael Mallett, *The Borgias: The Rise and Fall of the Most Infamous Family in History* (Academy, 1987) p. 110.
12. 'It seems to us that these men of his who surround him are little men who have small consideration for behaviour and have all the appearance of "marrani"' quoted in Bradford, 1976, p. 23.
13. Trans Lodovico Domenichi: Paolo Giovio, *Delle Istorie Del Suo Tempo: Prima Parte* (Rocca, 1565) p. 121.
14. Janet Ross, *Lives of the Early Medici: As Told in their Correspondence* (Chatto & Windus, 1910) p. 332.
15. Ibid.
16. Miles J. Unger, *Magnifico: The Brilliant Life and Violent Times of Lorenzo de' Medici* (Simon & Schuster, 2008) p. 435.
17. Raphael Sabatini, *The Life of Cesare Borgia: A History and some Criticisms* (Stanley Paul & Co, 1925), p. 60; Norwich., 2012, p. 252; Bradford, 1976, p. 26.

Chapter 3
1. Trans. Arnold Harris Mathew, Johannes Burchard, *The Diary of John Burchard of Strasburg translated from the Latin text: Volume 1 AD 1483–1492* (Francis Griffiths London, 1910) p. 54; Russell Chamberlain, *The Bad Popes* (Sutton, 2003) p. 169.
2. Steffano Infessura, *Diario della Citta di Roma* (Roma 1890) p. 282; Michael Mallet, *The Borgias: The Rise and Fall of the most Infamous Family in History* (Academy, 1987), p. 123.
3. Orestes Ferrara, *The Borgia Pope: Alexander the Sixth* (Sheed & Ward, 1942) p. 429.
4. *Ibid*, p. 125.
5. Chamberlain, 2003, p. 173; Mallett, 1987, p. 129; Meyer, 2013 p. 179.

Chapter 4
1. Bradford, 1976, p. 30.
2. Meyer, 2013, p. 181.
3. John Addington Symonds, *Renaissance in Italy: The Age of the Despots* (Smith, Elder & Co, 1912) p. 317.
4. Infessura, 1890, p. 283.
5. Sabatini, 1925, p. 94.
6. Gerard Noel, *The Renaissance Popes: Culture, Power and the Making of the Borgia Myth* (Constable, 2006) p. 122.
7. Trans. John Leslie Garner, Ferdinand Gregorovius, *Lucretia Borgia: According to Original Documents and Correspondance of her Day (originally published 1904)*, (D.Appleton & Co 1905), p. 72.
8. Bradford, 1976, p. 35.
9. de Roo, 1924, p. 505.
10. Gregorovius, 1905, p. 77.
11. Bradford, 1976, p. 37.
12. Letter from the 'Borgia family letters' within the Archivo Secreto Vaticano (A.A. ARM 5021, f 3rv, Viterbo, 31 (October 1493) as quoted in Bradford, 2005, p. 33.
13. Bradford, 2005, p. 35.
14. Gregorovius, 1905, p. 83.
15. Frieda, 2012, p. 184.
16. Michael Mallet & Christine Shaw, *The Italian Wars: 1494–1559* (Routledge 2014) p. 15.

17. Bradford, 1976, p. 43.
18. Trans. Geoffrey Parker, Johan Burchard, *At the Court of the Borgia: Being an account of the Reign of Pope Alexander VI written by his Master of Ceremonies* (The Folio Society, 1963) p. 119; Bradford, 1976, p. 47.
19. Bradford, 1976, p. 48.
20. Burchard, 1963, p. 120.
21. Meyer, 2013, p. 231.
22. Mallett & Shaw, 2012, p. 31.

Chapter 5
1. Bradford, 2005, p. 54.
2. Bradford, 1976, p. 56.
3. *Ibid*, p. 59; Meyer, 2013, p. 254–255.
4. Cloulas., 1989, p. 128.
5. Trans. John Leslie Garner, Ferdinand Gregorovius, *Lucretia Borgia; According to Original Documents and Correspondance of her day* (D. Appleton & Co, 1903) p. 104.
6. *"demum che la diceva, che dapoi era andata a miro, mai el ditto signor non havia usato con lei, perche 'l non poteva"* Marino Santo, *I Diarii di Marino Sanuto* volume 1 (F. Visentini, 1879) p. 649; quoted in Bradford, 2005, p. 59.
7. Marion Johnson, *The Borgias* (Macdonald 1981) p. 124.
8. Bradford, 1976, p. 61; Bradford, 2005, p. 61.
9. Hibbert, 2009 p. 106; Johnson, 1981, p. 124; Sabatini, 1925, p. 140.
10. Bradford, 1976, p. 62; Sabatini, 1925, p. 143.
11. Noel, 2006, p. 138.
12. Johannes Burchard, *Diarium sive Rerum Arbanarum Commentarii (1483–1506) Tome Second (1492–1499)* (Paris 1884) pp. 390–391; Burchard, 1963, p. 120. 1963) p. 17.
13. Meyer, 2013, p. 260.
14. Bradford, 1976, p. 66.
15. Trans. Sidney Alexander, Francesco Gucciardini, *The History of Italy* (Princeton University Press 1969) p. 124.
16. Hibbert, 2009, p. 79.

Chapter 6
1. *"Feria quarta, 14 dicti mensis februarii, Petrus Caldes, Perottus nincapatus, in camera SS. D. nostri serviens, qui jovis proxime preteriti 8 hujus, in nocte, cecidit in Tyberim non libenter, in eodem flumin repertus est, quo multa sunt per Urbem"* Johannes Burchard, *Diarium sive Rerum Urbanarum Commentarii (1483–1506) Tome Second (1492 – 1499)*, (Ernest Leroux 1884) pp. 432–433.
2. Trans. F. J. Sheed, Orestres Ferrara, *The Borgia Pope: Alexander VI* (Sheed & Ward, 1942) p. 254.
3. Trans. John Leslie Garner, Ferdinand Gregorovius, *Lucretia Borgia: According to Original Documents and Correspondence of her Day* (D Appleton & Co, 1902) p. 111.
4. Bradford, 2005, p. 72.
5. Francisco Rafael de Uhagon, Marques de Laurencin, *Relacion de los Festines que se celebraron en el Vaticano con motive de las bodas de Lucrecia Borgia con Don Alonso de Aragon, principe de Salerno, duqe de Biseglia, hijo natural de D. Alonso, rey de Napoles, ano 1498* (La Real Academia de la Historia, 1916) p. 85.
6. Bradford, 2005, p. 75.
7. Bradford, 1976, p. 74.
8. *"Pape thesaurarius generalis, celebravit missam solemnem in capella majore, Papa presented: interfuit etiam Rmus D. Cardinalis Valentinus qui a domenica ed Passione*

non fuit in capella. Alia acta sunt more solito" Johannes Burchard, *Diarium sive Rerum Urbanarum Commentarii (1483–1506) Tome Second (1492–1499)*, (Ernest Leroux 1884) pp. 448.

9. Trans. Andrew Scoble, Phillipe de Commynes, *The Memoirs of Philip de Commines, Lord of Argenton, Volume II* (London 1856) pp. 284.

10. Bradford, 1976, p. 76.

11. Johannes Burchard, *Diarium sive Rerum Urbanarum Commentarii (1483–1506) Tome Second (1492 – 1499)*, (Ernest Leroux 1884) pp. 492–493.

12. Victoria and Albert Museum, *Sword Scabbard* (http://collections.vam.ac.uk/item/O67243/sword-scabbard-unknown).

13. Bradford, 1976, p. 80.

14. Hibbert, 2009, pp. 124–125.

15. *Ibid* p. 125.

16. Bradford, 1976, p. 81.

17. *Ibid.*

18. Hibbert, 2009, p. 125.

19. Sabatini, 1925, p. 180.

20. Bradford, 1976, p. 82.

21. Sabatini, 1925, pp. 182–183.

22. Bradford, 1976, p. 95.

Chapter 7

1. E.L. Miron, *Duchess Derelict: A Study of the Life and Times of Charlotte d'Albret, Duchesse de Valentinois* (Stanley Paul & Co 1911) pp. 34–35.

2. *Ibid* p. 128.

3. Hibbert, 2009, p. 136.

4. *"Eadem die venit curso ex Francia, qui nuntiavit SS. D. nostro filium suum, olim Cardinalem Valentinum contraisse matrimonium cum Magnifica domina, a die presentis mensis et illud domenica ejusdem mensis consummasse et fecisse octo vices successive."* Johannes Burchard, *Diarium sive Rerum Urbanarum Commentarii 1483–1506, Tome Second (1492–1499)*, (Ernest Leroux, 1884) p. 532.

5. Hibbert, 2009, p. 136.

6. Trans. John Leslie Garner, Ferdinand Gregorovius, *Lucretia Borgia: According to Original Documents and Correspondence of Her Day* (D. Appleton & Co, 1903) pp. 117–118.

7. Trans. Bernard Wall, Maria Bellonci, *The Life and Times of Lucrezia Borgia* (Weidenfeld & Nicholson 1953) p. 114.

8. Bradford, 1976, p. 103.

9. Hibbert, 2009, p. 143.

10. Elizabeth Lev, *The Tigress of Forli: Renaissance Italy's Most Courageous and Notorious Countess, Caterina Sforza Riario de'Medici* (Houghton Mifflin Harcourt 2011) pp. 18–19.

11. *Ibid* p. 133.

12. Quoted in Bradford, 1976, p110; Bradford, 2005, p. 83.

13. *Ibid* p. 230.

Chapter 8

1. Cloulas., 1989, p. 177.

2. Bradford, 1976, p. 123.

3. Johann Burchard, *Diarium sive Rerum Urbanarum Comentarii (1483–1506) Tome Troisieme (1500 – 1506)* (Ernest Leroux 1885) p. 68 Burchard, 1963, p. 120. 1963) p. 183.

4. Johann Burchard, *Diarium sive Rerum Urbanarum Comentarii (1483–1506) Tome Troisieme (1500–1506)* (Paris 1885) pp.437; Bradford, 2005, p. 88.
5. Sanuto, 2005, p. 89.
6. Frieda, 2012, p. 227.

Chapter 9
1. Frieda, 2012, p. 230.
2. Bradford, 2005, p. 107.
3. Bellonci, 1939, p. 155.
4. Bradford, 2005, p. 121.
5. Sabatini, 1925, p. 308.
6. Bradford, 2005, pp. 122–123.
7. Sabatini, 1925, p. 312.
8. Bradford, 2005, p. 149.
9. Frieda, 2012, p. 239.
10. Trans. John Leslie Garner, Ferdinand Gregorovius, *Lucretia Borgia: According to Original Documents and Correspondence of her Day* (D Appleton & Company 1903) p. 248.
11. Frieda, 2012, p. 238.

Chapter 10
1. Oppenheimer, 2011, p. 129.
2. Bradford, 1976, pp. 180–181.
3. Bradford, 2005, p. 179.
4. Paul Strathern, *The Artist, The Philosopher and The Warrior* (Vintage 2010) p. 117.
5. *Ibid* p. 119.
6. Bradford, 1976, p. 192.
7. *Ibid* p. 194.
8. Oppenheimer, 2011, p. 148.
9. Niccolò Machiavelli, *The Prince* (Penguin 2003) pp. 56–57.

Chapter 11
1. Hugh Shankland, *The Prettiest Love Letters in the World: Letters Between Lucrezia Borgia & Pietro Bembo 1503–1519* (Collins Harvill 1987) p. 49.
2. *Ibid* p. 53.
3. *Ibid,* p. 55.
4. *Ibid,* p. 56.
5. *Ibid,* p. 57.
6. Bradford, 1976, p. 224.
7. Trans. F.J.Sheed, Orestes Ferrara, *The Borgia Pope: Alexander the Sixth* (Sheed & Ward 1942) p. 406.
8. Burchard, 1963, p. 120; Johannes Burchard, *Diarium sive Rerum Urbanarum Comentarii: Tome Troisieme (1500–1506)* (Ernest Leroux 1885) pp. 242–243.
9. Gucciardini, 1984, p. 166.
10. Charles Yriarte, *Cesare Borgia* (Aldus Publication 1947) p. 196.
11. Norwich., 2012, pp. 266–267.

Chapter 12
1. Bellonci, 1939, p. 210.
2. Bradford, 2005, p. 212.

3. Bradford, 1976, p. 281; Meyer, 2013, p. 406; Strathern, 2010, p. 366. Interestingly, this is quoted in many works on Cesare Borgia however no solid source has ever been given for it.
4. Bradford, 2005, p. 229.
5. Bellonci, 1939, p. 235.
6. Thomas Tuohy, *Herculean Ferrara: Ercole d'Este (1471–1505) and the Invention of a Ducal Capital* (Cambridge University Press 2002) p. 249.
7. Shankland, 1987, p. 98.
8. Bradford, 2005, p. 241.
9. Bradford, 1976, p. 285; Meyer, 2013, p. 407.
10. Bradford, 1976, p. 287; Strathern, 2010, p. 368; Samantha Morris, *Cesare Borgia in a Nutshell* (MadeGlobal 2016) p. 46; Yriarte, 1947, p. 219.
11. Sabatini, 1925, p. 450.
12. Salvador Martin Cruz, *Victoriano Juaristi Sagarzazu (1880–1949) El Ansia De Saber: Datos para una Biografia* (Gobierno de Navarra 2007) pp. 187–188.
13. Niccolò Machiavelli, *The Prince* (Penguin 2003) p. 27.

Chapter 13
1. Frieda, 2012, p. 282.
2. Edmund Gardner, *Dukes & Poets in Ferrara: A Study in the Poetry, Religion and Politics of the Fifteenth and Early Sixteenth Centuries* (E.P.Dutton & Co 1904) p. 512.
3. Bradford, 2005, p. 278.
4. Bellonci, 1939, p. 271.
5. Bradford, 2005, p. 283.
6. Bellonci, 1939, p. 280.
7. Michael Mallet & Christine Shaw, *The Italian Wars: 1494–1559* (Routledge 2014) p. 90.
8. Bradford, 2005, p. 305.
9. Mallet & Shaw, 2014, p. 90; Piero Pieri quotes these figures also in Piero Pieri, 'Consalvo di Cordova e le origini del modern esercito spagnolo' in *Fernado el Catolico e Italia* (Zaragoza: Institucion 'Fernando el Catolico' 1954) pp. 209–25.

Chapter 14
1. Trans. John Leslie Garner, Ferdinand Gregorovius, *Lucretia Borgia: According to Original Documents and Correspondance of her Day* (D.Appleton & Co 1905) p. 336.
2. Bradford, 2005, p. 318.
3. *Ibid*, p. 322.
4. Norwich., 2012, p. 279; Christopher Hibbert, *The Rise and Fall of the House of Medici* (Penguin 1979) p. 218.
5. Bradford, 2005, p. 330.
6. *Ibid.*

Chapter 15
1. Bellonci, 1939, p. 319.
2. Bradford, 2005, p. 346.
3. Trans. John Leslie Garner, Ferdinand Gregorovius, *Lucretia Borgia: According to Original Documents and Correspondance of her Day* (D.Appleton & Co 1905) p. 354.
4. Trans. John Leslie Garner, Ferdinand Gregorovius, *Lucretia Borgia: According to Original Documents and Correspondance of her Day* (D.Appleton & Co 1905) p. 355.
5. Bradford, 2005, p. 365.

Index